High Heels

AND A
HEAD TORCH

An avid reader during her childhood, Chelsea Duke went on to gain a good Honours degree in English Literature – aptly enough from the University of Reading. This was despite her dad's best efforts to get her to study engineering, business or 'something that would be useful in later life'. Being a people person, she gravitated towards a career in HR because it was less lonely than her childhood career plans of being an archivist or librarian.

But certain there was more to life than working nine to five, Chelsea decided to take off on a fifty-four-week solo round-the-world backpacking trip, which she describes at the most amazing thing she's ever done. Having been firmly bitten by the travel bug, and not yet feeling grown up enough to buy her own house, Chelsea now leads a semi-itinerant life, regularly upping sticks and travelling to far-flung places with little more than a visa, a sense of adventure and the obligatory rubber flip-flops. This is her first book.

High Heels

AND A

HEAD TORCH

THE ESSENTIAL GUIDE
FOR GIRLS WHO BACKPACK

Chelsea Duke

PAN BOOKS

First published 2009 by Pan Books
an imprint of Pan Macmillan Ltd
Pan Macmillan, 20 New Wharf Road, London N1 9RR
Basingstoke and Oxford
Associated companies throughout the world
www.panmacmillan.com

ISBN 978 0 330 47971 4

Copyright © Chelsea Duke 2009

The right of Chelsea Duke to be identified as the
author of this work has been asserted by her in accordance
with the Copyright, Designs and Patents Act 1988.

All rights reserved. No part of this publication may be
reproduced, stored in or introduced into a retrieval system, or
transmitted, in any form, or by any means (electronic, mechanical,
photocopying, recording or otherwise) without the prior written
permission of the publisher. Any person who does any unauthorized
act in relation to this publication may be liable to criminal
prosecution and civil claims for damages.

1 3 5 7 9 8 6 4 2

A CIP catalogue record for this book is available
from the British Library.

Printed by CPI Mackays, Chatham ME5 8TD

This book is sold subject to the condition that it shall not,
by way of trade or otherwise, be lent, re-sold, hired out,
or otherwise circulated without the publisher's prior consent
in any form of binding or cover other than that in which
it is published and without a similar condition including this
condition being imposed on the subsequent purchaser.
**Northamptonshire
Libraries & Information
Service
WW**

Visit www.panmacmillan.com to read more about all our books
and to buy them. You will also find features, author interviews and
news of any author events, and you can order any of our books

Askews

For Bryony.
Thank you for being so excited

Contents

Introduction

I realize I may not be completely unbiased when I say this BUT guidebooks are brilliant. When I was doing my planning, I may have underestimated the relative importance of guidebooks as compared to other, seemingly more vital arrangements for my year-long round-the-world trip such as, say, visas, flights and places to stay. While those items were, clearly, critical to the success of the trip, once I was out there on my own in the big wide world I found out that a decent guidebook was actually very important, as it not only made everything so much less bewildering but also helped out with the other stuff – like finding places to stay and knowing what the visa requirements were. My guidebooks became my constant friends and travelling companions, used so frequently that they acquired their own nicknames. My South American guidebook, for example, was referred to as The Bible since I seemed to live most of my travelling life According to The Word of The Book.

Following so carefully the tried-and-tested paths of countless previous travellers, seeing the same sights, eating in the same restaurants and sleeping in the same beds was not entirely the image I'd had of my trip when I started planning it. I saw myself as a free spirit, travelling the

1

world alone, seeking new friends and new experiences and seeing and doing some pretty exciting things on the way. Instead, I found myself slavishly consulting The Bible when planning my next meal, sightseeing trip or place to rest my weary bones.

Sometimes the conventionality of following the same route around the world as everyone else would become too much. At such times, I would indulge myself with a quiet and personal rebellion, deciding that I was perfectly capable of finding a decent and moderately priced restaurant by myself. I would then abandon the guidebook and set off in search of an elegant-yet-cost-effective dining establishment. I was usually cured of this presumptuousness by a couple of evenings of wandering through darkened streets peopled only by unsavoury-looking youths or bored-looking ladies of the night. (It has to be said that, if left to my own devices, I do seem to exhibit an unfortunate tendency to unerringly stumble into the red-light district in any given town. In Rio de Janeiro I surpassed myself and had the good fortune to stay in the heart of the local niche market for ladyboys of the night. It made for an interesting walk home from the pub, at least.)

These evenings of quiet rebellion tended to end with me either in a fast food burger bar, having failed to find anything remotely resembling a welcoming and wholesome restaurant, or with me consuming an unsatisfying meal of dubious quality and paying an extortionate price. Such experiences generally sent me scurrying back to the establishments recommended by the recently rejected guidebooks, tail between my legs. There's usually a reason why other travellers have been to the places listed in the guide-books, and that's because they're either worth seeing, worth eating at or worth staying in.

Eventually I realized that guidebooks were essential to my enjoyment of the trip and that if I wanted to eat reasonable food, see as much as I could in a short time and stay in the right area of town, it was quite a good idea to follow the books' advice, at least most of the time. The only other option (unless I particularly wanted to eat in red-light district kebab houses) was to go by recommendation either from fellow travellers or, even better, from the locals. The guidebook/recommendation combo worked well in most countries; the exception to this being India. There, the locals would recommend their brother-in-law-twice-removed's curry house as undisputedly the best in town regardless of the low hygiene standards and how many cockroaches had taken up residence.

Most of the time, my guidebooks happily provided me with all manner of useful information on practical matters such as how to get transport to and from the airport; how to avoid being murdered by a taxi driver in Delhi; exactly what the local speciality dish contains; which hostels actually do have hot showers as opposed to which hostels only claim they have hot showers; what to do if a Peruvian granny spits on your shoulder; and why the Chinese don't worry about queuing. There are, however, other subjects on which travel guides are entirely silent, but which nevertheless loom large in the life of girls who backpack. Things I wish I'd known before I went. Things like how to still feel glam with only one pair of decent shoes; survival tactics for cooking in hostel kitchens; the fact that, yes, head torches might look dumb at home but they're very useful on a pitch-black campsite in the middle of the Australian out-back; how to cope with sharing your room with strangers who snore (and worse); and how to deal with the realities of bush peeing and squat toilets.

Nothing I read before leaving home gave me any indication of the fact that I would quickly become comfortable with discussing my bowel movements with people I had met for the first time only five minutes earlier. I had no warning that I would learn the importance of rubber flip-flops the hard way (and believe me, they are not only important but I would venture to suggest actually critical – I'll tell you why a bit later), and nothing prepared me for quite how anal Australian customs officers can be. In fact, there's a whole lot of useful stuff that I learned on my way round the world. Things like being amazed at how many delicious meals you can make with pasta and a jar of tomato sauce; knowing what a South African means when they say they'll do something 'just now'; accepting that it's OK to wear slightly dirty clothes as long as they don't actually smell; and figuring out how to buy toothpaste in Argentina.

So, this book is for all the girlie travellers of the world. If you're in your late teens taking a gap year or you've recently finished uni and you're seeing a bit of the world before you settle down, well done. If you're a bit older, then well done as well. It'll be brilliant. I hope we might run into each other. I'll be the one in the sparkly flip-flops.

Chapter One

FIRST THINGS FIRST

After you've done the important stuff like booking your tickets, buying your guidebooks and making your family and friends jealous by showing them pictures of the beautiful beaches upon which you're shortly going to be soaking up the sun, you'll eventually have to start thinking about what to take with you and what else you need to do before you go. It's quite a weird concept to get your head round, isn't it? Basically, before you leave home you've got to pack everything you're going to wear and need for a year (or however long it is you're going for). Now I don't know about you, but being famously indecisive I've been known to take two dresses, three pairs of shoes, several sets of underwear, half a tonne of make-up and my entire jewellery collection just for a one-night stay to attend a posh do. The idea of having to think about what you might want to wear for the whole of the next year is a bit daunting, and that's before you've thought about any special equipment you might need.

Then there's the space issue as well. Given the likely size of the backpack you'll be taking away on your long trip, the task facing you is a bit like trying to imagine fitting the contents of your double wardrobe into a bathroom cabinet. Sadly, it's unlikely that you'll be able to take with you absolutely everything you want to take. Those gorgeous knee-high boots you got for your last birthday that you always pull in? They're never going to fit in your backpack, or at least if they do not much else is going in with them. Buck naked except for the boots is undoubtedly a good look on certain occasions, but it's just not going to work on the Inca Trail. Some tough decisions will have to be made. The sad fact is that the average backpack is probably smaller than your shoe cupboard, but try to think of it as part of the adventure and the perfect opportunity to declutter your life a little bit. Plus, coming home and being reunited with your favourite heels or your best top will give you something to look forward to. If you can't fit everything you want in, don't panic. If you leave something out and then find that you absolutely cannot live without it, you'll almost certainly be able to buy it on the way round – at some point. If your first stop is in the middle of nowhere, make certain you've got everything critical before you leave home.

GETTING YOUR KIT

This isn't like your average holiday. This time, you're not going to be able to get away with shoving some bits in a suitcase the night before you get on the plane and assuming it's going to be OK. You can try, but you might find yourself in a bit of bother later. It's much better just to get organized before you go.

Firstly, do a bit of planning. Talk to any friends who've done some travelling and start checking out camping and travel shops to get an idea of what kit's available. There are also lots of travel websites you can use, which, like travel agents, might be able to provide you with suggested packing lists. Get hold of some of these, have a read, have a think about the sorts of activities you want to do and the weather you'll be doing them in and you'll start to get an idea of what clothes and equipment you'll need. Think comfort as well as what will look good. If you're going somewhere cold, make sure you've got a thermal vest and a woolly hat. OK, so they're not that glam but trust me, you'll look a lot more attractive if you're snug and warm than if you're blue, shivering and have a shiny, red, runny nose. The Rudolph look is not in this year.

After you've done some of this thinking, start writing lists. Lists will, in all likelihood, become central to your existence in the days prior to the long-anticipated first flight. I thought I was a list person before I started trying to sort out spending a year with only one small backpack; it could only get worse. In the run-up to departure I became Listzilla. I had lists of where to go, lists of what buy, lists of what to pack, lists of what still had to be booked, lists of what I still had to do before I left home. I even had lists of lists. The good thing with lists is that you don't have to worry about remembering everything (or forgetting something) because it's all written down. Lists are very reassuring. They also help to give you the impression that you're far more organized than you actually are and that you do know what you're doing, which always makes you feel good.

Tempting as it may be to rush out and stock up on shiny new kit, the time to get the credit card out in the world of camping shops and travel stores is *after* you've done your thinking. With a bit of prior exploration and some lists behind you, the array of equipment on offer will be less daunting and you'll be less likely to spend a fortune on something you don't really need. Camping shops clearly aren't as exciting as designer malls to shop in, but they're kind of a necessity in this situation and there might even be the added bonus of bumping into some totty in the form of a rugged outdoors type. You never know, ask his advice about head torches and he might end up inviting you out for a drink.

Choosing your equipment

Choosing equipment might seem a bit scary simply because there's so much of it on offer, all of which makes fantastically wordy claims about what appears to be the outdoor equipment equivalent of superhuman powers. Before buying anything, really think about what you need it for and pay attention to the advice you've read. If you're going to Australia and New Zealand in the summer, do you really need a sleeping bag that will keep you warm down to temperatures of minus 20, or will one that'll keep you warm just down to freezing do? Also, don't assume that a head torch is a head torch is a head torch. How many different varieties can there be? I hear you ask. Answer: about twelve, and I chose the wrong one because I hadn't done my research. Just so that you don't do the same, here's my advice: get one with LEDs instead of conventional bulbs. LEDs don't need replacing as often and LEDs don't break when you drop the torch. Which you will.

It's only for things like backpacks, head torches and sleeping bags that you're faced with a bewildering array of options. Other kit will be a bit easier to select, if only because there's less choice. You'll be able to stock up on essentials that you probably never knew you needed before. Things like travel towels (which allegedly fold up really, really small and dry really, really quickly), a sarong, a washing line that doesn't need pegs, a penknife, a miniature sewing kit, rechargeable batteries, super-concentrate travel wash (that can be used to wash you, your clothes and even dirty dishes) and a special travel first-aid kit with its own syringes and lots of stuff for sunburn and upset stomachs. You should also remember to pack a small shoulder bag or daypack for carrying things like your camera, passport, money, a bottle of water and some suncream around with you when you're sightseeing, as the last thing you want to end up doing is traipsing up and down mountainsides visiting Buddhist temples with your entire year's worth of clothes and essentials strapped to your back.

Buying your kit is one of those occasions in life when size really does matter. That backpack might look quite big from the point of view of something you have to carry around, but it's quite small when looked at from the point of view that it has to fulfil the combined functions of your wardrobe, shoe cupboard and bathroom cabinet. Even though you're on a budget, it might be worth paying the extra £20 for a sleeping bag that squashes up to four inches shorter than its cheaper cousin. An extra four inches (as I'm sure we all know) can make a huge difference to your general pleasure. In backpacking terms it could be the difference between two T-shirts or three, or even the difference between taking some heels and not taking some heels.

THE IMPORTANCE OF A HEAD TORCH

Yes, I know they look ridiculous and wearing one will ruin your hair, but if you're going to be camping at any point during your trip, you will need a head torch. Simple as that. Firstly, it's almost impossible to enjoy your bedtime read in a tent without the benefit of a head torch. The reasons for this are twofold. Number One – if your torch is not on your head but in your hand, you have to balance precariously and uncomfortably on the elbow that belongs with your torch-holding hand so as to leave the other hand free for page turning. When camping on rough ground this can be extremely painful. Number Two – if you don't want to hold your torch, the alternative is to grip it in your teeth. That's not too great for your teeth but it also gives you jaw ache and makes you dribble. Attractive. Secondly, and far more practically, it is impossible to pitch a tent in the dark one-handed. Head torches also come in very handy when attempting to cook anything on an unlit campsite after dark, since the light from a gas ring isn't really all that illuminating.

Even if you're not camping, you might want to think

about getting a head torch if you're a reader as they come in quite handy when staying in hostels without reading lights. A head torch means you don't have to irritate all your dorm mates by leaving the light on and you don't have to get out of bed to turn the light off when you've finished reading.

Choosing your backpack

Selecting your backpack itself is going to be one of the most important decisions you make in terms of kit. It has to be comfortable for you to carry, so do make sure you try it on in the shop, and do up all the straps, and adjust them if necessary to get the best fit, and only then decide if it's comfortable and if it's the right size for you.

You also need to think about how you're going to access your stuff once it's inside the backpack. With a traditional rucksack which opens at the top, you stack things one on top of the other. What this means in practice is that invariably you'll have to take everything out every time you want anything as the item you want, no matter what it is, will always be at the bottom. It matters not that you put it near the top, it's just one of those inalienable rules of life that the very thing you want at any given point in time migrates to the bottom of the rucksack. It's much the same principle which dictates that the freshest loaf of bread is always right at the back of the supermarket shelf and you will have to move enough loaves to feed a small Third World nation before you can get the one that's going to last more than ten minutes without going stale. Instead of having to rummage around for ages looking for things, for ease of access I'd recommend one of those packs with the zip that goes all the way around the outside so that the front peels back like a lid and you can see pretty much everything inside without too much rummaging.

Determining the size of backpacks is a bit strange as they're sold by capacity, measured in litres. When selecting my backpack I was swayed by the clearly superior knowledge of the sales assistant, whose contribution to my general confusion was to assure me that it was inadvisable for women to carry a pack larger than 60 litres.

It sounded sensible but the problem was that, in common with most women, I have no idea about volume at all since it's a three-dimensional concept. The reason we don't get this is apparently because the female brain isn't wired to think in that way. That's why when we're reading maps we have to turn them round to face the same way as we're going. Applying myself to the tricky volume question in relation to the great backpack purchase meant that trying to imagine what 60 litres might look like when converted to a pile of clothing was pretty much a lost cause. The only thing I could think of that came in litres was bottles of lemonade; 60 bottles of lemonade stacked side by side would cover quite a sizeable area, I thought. That sounds OK, I thought. I neglected to think that it's not the bottles which are measured in litres, but their contents; 60 litres of lemonade poured into one container takes up a whole lot less space than 60 litre-bottles of lemonade.

14

The best thing to do is not to think about what it means but just treat it as a relative term: 50 litres means smaller than 60 litres. If you're worried about the space, get the biggest one you can sensibly carry. Whatever you end up with, even if it means your available backpack space is smaller than you may have wished, it is going to be sharing your adventures with you for a year and you will grow to love it. I promise.

DOs and DON'Ts for getting your kit

- DO make sure you try backpacks on for size and fit before buying one.
- DO enjoy and celebrate lists. They will become central to your existence and your life will not be considered complete without at least six lists being in simultaneous operation at any given time.
- DO your research before you go shopping – it helps to avoid injury to your budget by buying more kit than you need or kit that does things you don't need it to.
- DON'T buy your backpack in a sale – if you do a trial pack and it's just not big enough, you might not be able to take it back.
- DO consider paying a bit extra to get something smaller – backpacking is a case where bigger is not necessarily better.
- DO invest in a head torch – it might look ridiculous at home but you'll be the one laughing when you're in the middle of the Australian outback, it's pitch black and everyone else is trying, and failing, to put their tent up one-handed.

WHAT TO PACK

Once you've bought all your shiny new kit, the next thing to think about is clothes and shoes. What you need to take with you will depend on where you're going and what you'll be doing, as well as being restricted by the space available to you. If you're doing the standard backpacker route round the world – Thailand, Fiji, New Zealand, Australia, America, home (or reverse) – your travelling time is likely to involve little more than a succession of beaches and bars interspersed with a few extreme sports. You'll be able to get away with taking not much more than some jeans and a couple of T-shirts, plus a couple of decent outfits to go out in and some swimwear. You've probably even got room for some heels if you want and you're unlikely to need the washing line or the penknife (except possibly to open beer bottles).

If, however, you've opted for something a little more involved, you'll need appropriate clothes. If you're trekking to visit Thai hill tribes or walking the Inca Trail, for example, you'll need walking boots and reasonable walking trousers. If you're going to India or off the main tourist track anywhere else in Asia, you'll need clothes which cover you up; South East Asia is populated by modest people and they don't appreciate displays of Western flesh. In addition to the risk of offending the locals, if you're in India and not wearing something resembling a tent that completely disguises all your womanly bits, you're reasonably likely to encounter groping hands when you're in public places like markets or train stations. Best avoided, really. If you're planning on working at all during your trip then you'll need some working clothes – either some black trousers and a white top if you're planning on waitressing or getting a bar job, or some scruffy clothes you don't mind getting dirty if you're planning on doing gardening, fruit picking or farm work.

Clothes

When choosing which clothes to take with you the key words are practicality, coordination and comfort. You haven't got all that much space, so take clothes that work well with each other. Ideally, if you've got two pairs of trousers, you want to take T-shirts that go with both of them. You don't want any items which you can only wear with one other item in your pack if you can help it. Apart from the fact that sometimes it's inconvenient to have to ferret around in your pack to find the only two things that go together, the fact that if one of them needs washing then that's a whole outfit out of commission is also pretty annoying. Think clothes that multitask; those trousers with the zip-off legs that become shorts are pretty useful, and if you can do shorts (I can't, or rather won't – hideous knees), then they're great because obviously they take up a lot less space than trousers so you can probably fit in a few more pairs, giving yourself a bit more choice.

Black is generally a good choice as it coordinates with most things. Think very carefully about taking white or other light-coloured clothes. Yes, white does showcase your tan fantastically, but it also shows the dirt rather well too. Plus, if you've got fair skin and need to use a lot of sun cream, that's one thing that doesn't mix well with white. It produces greasy yellow smears on any pale clothing it touches – neither attractive to look at nor easy to wash out and, as you'll find out in Chapter Four, doing laundry on your trip isn't always quite as easy as popping it in the washing machine and letting the machine do all the hard work, like you do at home.

If you're camping, light-coloured trousers are a really bad idea as you will always (and I do mean always) get either mud stains or grass stains (or quite possibly both) on your trousers each time you put up a tent. In fact, green or khaki combat is a good choice for camping for precisely this reason. Take a leaf out of the book of Elizabethan prostitutes – they used to wear green so that the grass stains wouldn't show. It's a useful trick, and not just for putting up tents.

When choosing the clothes to take with you, think about where you're going as well. If you will be spending the majority of your time in hot countries then one jumper or a light fleece is probably going to be enough. If you're going somewhere in winter, though, you might need a few more layers than that. When thinking about underwear, don't go into autopilot and pack clean socks and knickers for each day like your mum used to tell you to do when you were little. Again, if you're somewhere hot you're going to be wandering around in sandals or flip-flops most days, so you just won't need as many pairs of clean socks as you do clean knickers – assuming you like to wear clean knickers every day. Alternatively you could go commando, then you won't have to worry about packing any at all. In fact, that's not a bad space-saving idea. Why didn't I think of that before I went?

Choosing clothes suitable for going out in but which won't be ruined by being squashed into your backpack is the key to looking great even though you've only got a tiny selection of things to wear. Fabric, colour and style are important. To make you feel good when you go out, choose a colour that really suits you and a flattering style that makes the most of your body shape. Then comes the more difficult bit – make sure it's in a fabric that won't crease. Anything with a high percentage of Lycra is great as you can completely screw it up, but once you put it on the creases don't show. Cotton and linen, on the other hand, are definitely not a good idea. They'll look like a three-dimensional map of a mountain range after being in your backpack for less than five minutes, never mind five weeks. As with the rest of your clothes, think about multitasking outfits. Think colour that coordinates. As an absolute minimum your 'going out' top needs to go with your jeans, as well as whatever you've planned to wear it with (like some decent trousers or a skirt, or maybe hot pants if you've got good legs).

If you've got the backpack space, definitely take a skirt with you. It'll mean that you've got something you can put on that will instantly make you feel more feminine and sexy. And, of course, if you've managed to get a good tan a skirt will show off your legs beautifully. If space is a problem but you want to have more than one outfit option for the evenings, then go with a skirt or trousers in black or white and take a couple of different coloured tops. Tops take up less packing space than bottoms so they're the easiest to vary.

Be warned – ignore the advice of the 'what to pack' lists at your peril. I didn't originally pack a hat or gloves. Yes, they were listed in every single 'what to pack' list I'd read. No, I didn't think I'd need them. What I failed to realize was that going to Ushuaia (the town they sail to Antarctica from – spot the huge clue there as to what the prevailing temperature is likely to be) during the winter would actually be freezing, and not just a little chilly as I had (wrongly) assumed. If you're cold in bed at night, wearing a woolly hat really does warm you up. On the down side, it does absolutely nothing for your hair, but sometimes it's a choice between looking good and being comfortable, and when you're shivering uncontrollably and unable to sleep because you're so cold, personally, I'd go with the hat. And I did. Actually, it was so cold that I ended up buying myself a hat and wearing it 24/7 for about four days, which meant the bad hair didn't really notice. No one even saw my hair and I also saved a bit on shampoo because there really was no point in washing my hair just to shove it all under a woolly hat for it to get greasy again in super quick time. Every cloud has a silver lining.

Finally, try to choose stuff you know you look good in; it'll help you relax, which is important when you're spending a fair bit of your time meeting new people. But, having said that, don't take anything you're really attached to because there is some degree of risk it might get either damaged or irretrievably dirty while you're travelling and it may not ever be quite the same again. Similarly, while it's tempting to go and buy a whole lot of new things, they may well get ruined so it might not be worth the expense. And just remember, £20 NOT spent on a new top at home will keep you in cocktails for a week in Bangkok. Sometimes it's worth the sacrifice.

Make-up

Take a couple of items of make-up with you, even if you're not going to be wearing it every day. It'll make you feel a little bit more dressed up when you go out. If desperate, you can do something just with Vaseline (use it as a lipgloss, or use a tiny dab to tidy up your eyebrows), but for evenings out you really do want a little bit more than that. I made the mistake of starting off without packing any make-up. In fact, I laughed at my sister's expression of horror at my pronouncement that I wasn't going to be taking any make-up with me.

'None at all?' she asked, in a tone that sounded as if I'd just announced I'd be travelling round the world naked.

'None,' I confirmed. 'I don't need it.'

Since the differences between me and my sister are essentially that a) I can go out for the evening without first having to try on every single item of clothing in the wardrobe, and b) I don't have to have a bra to match every single colour top I own, I genuinely thought she was being overly girlie and I could survive perfectly happily without make-up. After all, for a good part of the year I was going to be camping and there's never a mirror or good light in a tent, is there? I soon found out, though, that make-up just makes you feel a little bit better about yourself, especially if you've not got your favourite boots or your awesome new top. Make-up is not called war paint for nothing – sometimes it does make you feel like you can go out there and face the world, which is what you need when you're spending a lot of time in bars full of strangers. Apologies to feminists everywhere, but it does. I don't like admitting I'm wrong, though, so since I was on the other side of the world and I figured she'd never find out, I didn't tell my sister that just this once, she was right and I was wrong. So, sssshhhhhh, keep it quiet, please.

If you are intending to take make-up with you, be warned – make-up and hot weather are not a good combination. Things melt or go all sticky and generally yuck. Mascara is particularly bad (which is why tinting your eyelashes before you go could be a good plan) but lipstick can also get a bit sloppy. In really hot places, if you have access to a kitchen you can always keep your make-up in the fridge, which will stabilize it even after it's got a bit gooey. However, do be prepared for the possibility that hot weather might completely ruin items of make-up so don't take your really expensive stuff with you. Instead, stock up on the cheap and cheerful before you leave home, and to save space and weight, try to limit yourself to a few items that will complement the clothes you've got with you.

22

Jewellery

A small selection of jewellery can be great to accessorize with. It doesn't necessarily have to take up too much space but, like make-up, can really make you feel as though you've dressed up and made an effort for the occasion. You might want to consider taking with you a couple of necklaces, a couple of pairs of earrings and maybe some rings or bracelets – but don't take any family heirlooms, just in case they go walkabout. As with your clothes, if it's really special, leave it at home. Keep any jewellery you do take with you all together in a small box or tin to keep it from getting tangled up with everything else in your backpack and to avoid losing the smaller items. Again, choose colours and styles that go with as many of the clothes you're taking as possible and also look out for jewellery to buy as souvenirs or gifts as you travel round. I didn't originally take jewellery with me, but I did add some on the way round. Again, it's amazing how much more girlie you feel when you've got a few small accessories to make your evening appearance differ from how you look during the day.

If you've got any body piercings, you need to take spare parts with you. Sod's Law says that if you are going to lose the ball from your ball closure ring, or if your jewellery is going to break, you can pretty much guarantee that it will do so in a place where you've got no hope of buying a replacement any time soon. Whether it's three days into a ten-day trip through the Australian outback, when you're halfway round the Inca Trail, or, as happened to me, just as you're about to board a fifteen-hour flight, it's a major pain. In an emergency, if you lose a fastening you can sometimes improvise with a bit of sticking plaster or Sellotape to hold the jewellery in place until you're able to sort it out but it won't look good and, depending on where the piercing is, it might not be all that comfortable. The more tender parts of your anatomy definitely do not benefit from the liberal application of sticky tape. Certain piercings will close up in an extremely short time period without jewellery in them, so if you don't want to have the pain and expense of getting re-pierced, make sure you've got spares.

JUST IN CASE YOU'RE INTERESTED – HERE'S WHAT I PACKED ON MY FIRST TRIP

When a well-travelled friend told me that he'd only taken three T-shirts with him when he spent a year going round the world, I was incredulous. I mean, can you imagine? Just three T-shirts – for the whole year? For a start it means that in all your photos you're wearing the same outfit. I'll do better than that, I thought confidently to myself. When it came to packing time it became clear that actually, no, I wasn't going to do better than that. By the time I'd inserted into my 60-litre backpack my brand new, clean and as yet unmuddied walking boots (yes, the ones that should have been thoroughly muddied before they ever left English shores) and an industrial-sized washbag stuffed with enough suncream, malaria tablets, tampons and condoms to sink a small battleship, there wasn't a whole lot of room for anything

---

else. I needed clothes and equipment for activities as diverse as camping in South America, trekking to visit Thai hill tribes, doing voluntary work on a game reserve in South Africa, walking the Inca Trail, surviving a month in India and working as an outback barmaid. I had to take kit for all of that as well as kit suitable for the more normal backpacker beach and bar bus tours in the Antipodes. Something had to give and it wasn't going to be the walking boots (or the condoms).

Reluctantly, and in some haste (having left everything to the last minute), I concluded that vanity would have to take a back seat; practicality was the name of the packing game. So it was that in addition to my kit and equipment, I left home, for a year, with:

- Two pairs of cotton quick-drying trousers (one khaki, one grey) and one pair of jeans.
- Three T-shirts (black, green and brown).
- One jumper (black) and one fleece (black and grey).
- One thermal vest.
- A waterproof jacket and waterproof trousers (of the giant blue condom variety so vividly and accurately evoked in Bill Bryson's *Notes from a Small Island*).
- A swimming costume.
- A waterproof sarong.
- Three pairs of socks and six pairs of knickers.
- Walking boots, walking shoes and the ugliest pair of Velcro sandals known to man.

You'll notice immediately that this wasn't the most colourful wardrobe in the world. You'll also notice that I didn't have any heels or in fact any item of clothing that was remotely girlie. I did, however, have three pairs of shoes. Walking shoes and walking boots may seem a little excessive. In my defence, I needed the boots for things like the Inca Trail but I also thought that sightseeing around cities in heavy boots might be a bit tedious so I wanted the walking shoes for that. I'd packed in a rush and packed for practicality alone. There's a reason why that's not a good idea.

Shoes

Choosing your shoes may be even more difficult than choosing your clothes. If you're going to be hiking, your own boots are essential – some pieces of equipment you can hire, but hiking boots is not one I'd recommend. Do you really want to put your feet into something several hundred other people have sweated into? Thought not. To be comfortable, you really need your own boots and you need them to be worn in. If you've bought new boots to wear on your trip, don't do what I did and think that 'wearing them in' means wearing them round town a couple of times. Wearing them in means walking long distances in them, and walking in them frequently. Anything less and you risk ending up like me after the Inca Trail – in agony, covered in blisters and unable to wear anything but flip-flops for a week despite the cold.

As you'll have noticed from my packing list, I didn't originally pack any evening shoes. As a result, I found myself lurking moodily in the corners of bars feeling inferior, having realized that I am not at my sociable, con-

versational and flirtatious best when clad in baggy, many-
pocketed, quick-drying travel trousers in an unflattering
but enormously practical shade of khaki green, teamed
with those exceptionally ugly Velcro sandals. Undeniably
sensible attire but definitely not sexy. Strangely enough it
was the lack of girlie shoes that actually bothered me more
than the unflattering trousers. I'd never quite got it before,
but backpacking showed me that there most definitely is
something in this foot fetish thing after all. Put on some
fabulous shoes and you really do feel like you can conquer
the world. You're probably not going to be packing your
Jimmy Choos in your rucksack, but something a little girlie
in the shoe line is definitely required.

Some strappy sandals could be a great addition to the
backpack if you've got the space. There really is nothing
like high heels to make you feel feminine and sexy, and
strappy sandals are fab. They won't go out of shape too
much by being squashed into a backpack and they also
won't take up all that much room. If you can, choose a pair
you can wear with jeans as well as with a skirt (if you're
taking one with you) as then you've got two possible outfits
for going out in. You can always dress the jeans up with a
nice top and a touch of make-up. Unfortunately for me, I
just didn't have the space for heels at all, even little ones, but
I found the next best thing: sparkly flip-flops. Minimal
packing space required but they take an outfit from day to
evening, even jeans. They work especially well if you're in
hot countries. You can dance the night away without your
feet hurting at all. If you're in a cold country though, flip-

flops or strappy sandals maybe aren't so great. You just might find yourself in a nightclub in jeans and your hiking boots as I did in Buenos Aires, Argentina. Luckily there were thirty of us in the same boat – I'm sure we were a curious sight strutting our funky stuff in heavy boots, but on the plus side we got as much space on the dance floor as we wanted – everybody else was too scared to come near us in case we stood on their feet.

Try to resist the temptation to take too many pairs of shoes with you. Really, one pair of sensible shoes for walking and the like, one pair of shoes to go out in and one pair of flip-flops or similar should probably do. I know it's hard, but try.

THE SIGNIFICANCE AND USES OF THE RUBBER FLIP-FLOP

A pair of flip-flops wasn't on my original packing list. In fact, I didn't even own a pair of flip-flops before I left home. Failing to pack flip-flops was A Serious Error. Along with a head torch and a credit card, rubber flip-flops are the item never to leave home without when you're backpacking. They're more user-friendly than sandals because they can be removed easily. That's an important consideration if you're in Thailand and having to take your shoes off every time you want to go into a temple, or a shop, or a restaurant, or even an Internet café. Trust me, you really don't want to be having to undo and do up your sandals fifteen-plus times a day.

And, if you're camping, the only thing more annoying than having to stop and take your shoes off every time you go into your tent is constantly having to sweep out the dirt, leaves and twigs you drag in with you if you don't take your shoes off. The rubber flip-flop specifically is even more useful than the ordinary flip-flop for this purpose because of course it's waterproof and therefore can be left outside your tent in the rain without suffering any ill effects.

In fact, the rubber flip-flop is an item that really multi-tasks and amply justifies its required packing space. The rubber flip-flop, quite simply, is:

- Ideal for camping – being easily removable at the tent door.
- Ideal for flinging at snorers – to prompt the 'nudge and roll over' reaction.
- Ideal for use on boat trips – where you might have to climb out of the boat and wade a short distance through the sea.
- Ideal for Thailand and other countries where removal of your shoes before entering a building is considered courteous.

And, as we'll find out later, the rubber flip-flop is also, unexpectedly, a critical piece of equipment when dealing with matters of the bathroom.

Other stuff

There are also a whole bunch of incidentals you'll need to take in addition to your clothes, your shoes and your kit. This stuff is pretty important: things like medication, toiletries, tampons and condoms. On the tampons question, how many to take is really up to you. I've seen girls with half a backpack full of nothing but tampons. If it's going to be an issue for you, take plenty. I took very seriously the dire and oft repeated warnings in guidebooks that tampons are very hard to obtain in some countries, and I was pleased I did. If you can cope with sanitary towels then you won't have a problem, but do be aware that the potential for nasty smells increases when in hot weather so pack some feminine wipes to keep yourself feeling fresh.

If you're not a sanitary towels fan then beware because the guidebooks, as is often the case, were right. In countries like South America and Asia, sanitary towels are pretty much all you're going to get so if you don't like them, make sure you pack enough tampons to see you through. Don't forget you can always replenish your stocks in more civilized locations like Australia, though, so you don't need to try to carry an entire year's worth straight off.

Condoms are critical, so don't forget them. You definitely don't want to be without one when you need it as you're unlikely to know your partner that well if it's someone you've met while you've been travelling, possibly only hours earlier. You also don't want to be trying to buy them in a strange language, and in some countries (again, South-

East Asia and some Catholic countries) they're only available in vending machines in the Gents, not the Ladies, since it's assumed that ladies won't wish to be engaging in such activities. I'm assuming you're the kind of girl who likes to be in control so you don't want to leave it all up to him. Plus, like me, you might just prefer to trust to British safety standards rather than anything else.

Medication is a very personal thing but if you have prescriptions, check your itinerary and try to make sure you've got enough to last at least until America or the Antipodes. It's generally easier to go to a doctor and get a repeat prescription in an English-speaking country and they'll be familiar with most of the brands from home as well.

DOs and DON'Ts on what to pack:

- DO think about what you're going to be doing and what clothes you'll need for that, that will also be comfortable and look good.
- DO try to pick clothes that multitask and coordinate with more than one other item.
- DO pack according to your itinerary. Take enough medication, tampons and condoms to see you through to a country where you can easily restock. At the same time, remember that you can buy things like shampoo and shower gel abroad, so you don't need to try to carry a gallon of it.
- DON'T take a lot of white or light-coloured clothes if you're going to be covering yourself in suncream fifteen times a day *or* if you're going to be doing a lot of camping.

- DON'T worry about taking as many pairs of socks as knickers if you're going somewhere hot as you won't need them.

- DON'T ignore the advice of the 'what to pack' lists without very good reason. You might regret it. Three freezing cold nights in Argentina and boy, did I regret it.

- DO take a skirt and/or heels and/or make-up – something to make you feel a bit girlie and sexy.

- DON'T take expensive make-up with you in case the heat ruins it. Instead stock up on cheap and cheerful versions before you leave home (make sure you're not allergic though – you won't look so attractive blotchy and swollen).

- DO just laugh and add it to your list of backpacker stories if you find yourself going clubbing in hiking boots.

FINDING THE MOST USELESS ITEM IN THE BACKPACK

I did my packing in a panic and ended up prioritizing practicality above all else. You probably realized straight away that wasn't a good idea. You'd be right. Practicality to the point of fascism is definitely not the way to go when packing for a round-the-world trip. Yes, there is a bit of a crisis in terms of space, but you still have to allow yourself some indulgences. Don't be tempted to do the same as me and leave out everything that isn't entirely 100 per cent useful.

However, despite my excessively practical packing and being very short of space, there were still some things that I'd packed just because they were listed in the 'what to pack' lists, and they sounded important – but to be honest, I wasn't entirely sure exactly what I was going to do with them. That's why it's important to think about what you're going to be doing and to pack accordingly. If something in the backpack isn't useful then it might not be worth keeping. If you're short of space, unloading stuff that's not justifying its packing space as you go lightens the load and creates more room for souvenirs (or extra make-up).

I pondered getting rid of a few things on the way round, but there were three items in particular that I really thought were quite useless for large chunks of the year. Contenders for the prestigious 'Most Useless Item in the Backpack' award are:

Contender #1: the compass

There was a point in my backpacking life when I thought that the compass would be the item I carted around all year without using it at all. All the 'what to pack' lists tell you to take one. I didn't really think I'd need one. After all, I'm not an outdoorsy, let's-hike-along-this-unmarked-trail-on-this-moor type of person, so I was dubious about its value, didn't have one, didn't have any spare cash to buy one and so didn't. Then one of my housemates gave me one as a leaving present. It was quite small and it seemed a little silly to leave it behind having been given it, so it went in. It didn't see the light of day for eight months. Then I arrived in Beijing.

When I visited Beijing it was a city in transition, being spruced up and aggressively modernized in the name of the Olympics. Traditional one-storey courtyard housing was being bulldozed to make way for new multi-lane roads and sleek tower blocks. Maps were out of date as soon as they were printed. My guidebooks were not much help at all in some areas of the city because most of what was in them was no more. Not only that, but unlike Thailand where street signs are helpfully written in both English and Thai, signs in Beijing are in Mandarin only. It took me a good couple of weeks before I could recognize the three characters that in combination denote an Internet café. Further than that I was unable to progress. Luckily for me, after a few bewildering days spent getting frequently lost, I had the good fortune to meet a fellow English traveller who understood the value of the compass. Beverley pointed out to me that it doesn't matter if the roads on the map aren't the same as the roads on the ground; it's the direction of travel that's critical. As long as you're heading in roughly the right direction, you'll get there in the end. What I learnt was that even if you're a city girl, a compass might come in handy.

My compass goes almost everywhere with me now. Even at home. I've used it to help me find my way around London and it's proved far more reliable than my usual method of coming out of the Underground, looking at the map, deciding which way I should be going and then setting off in the opposite direction as I'm usually standing on the opposite side of the street to the one I think I'm on, so my idea of where I'm supposed to be going is basically backwards. The compass also came to my rescue in Hong Kong when I ridiculously got completely disorientated inside an underground department store which was, for some reason, also the exit of a Kowloon subway station. I was just going round and round in circles for a good ten minutes. I was starting to despair of ever seeing daylight again when I remembered I could use the compass to lead me out safely. I wonder if I'm the only person ever to have had to navigate their way through the lingerie department?

Since it did prove to be useful in the end I'm glad I didn't throw out the compass. It isn't, however, infallible. A cautionary tale: the compass is only as good as the person interpreting the map accompanying it. I met backpackers who had repeatedly got completely lost when trying to find their way around various Middle Eastern cities, despite following the 'correct' direction as indicated on the compass. The reason for the confusion was that they were using maps bought locally. In the Middle East, the arrow printed on the map may not point north, as you might expect, but instead may indicate the direction of Mecca.

Contender #2: the waterproof trousers

It is possible to buy waterproof trousers from camping and travel shops that look like normal trousers and are breathable. If you're going to be doing a lot of walking, it's definitely worth investing in these. I didn't. Instead, I purchased the plastic pull-on-over-your-normal-trousers variety because they were cheaper and I didn't think I'd need to use them all that much. And indeed, I didn't use them all that much. This was largely because they looked ridiculous. They were unattractively unsuitable for my typically feminine shape (for which read: I have hips and a noticeable bum), and because they're made of plastic they're spectacularly non-breathable. Thus, wearing them to keep the rain off was completely pointless as I just sweated profusely inside them. Personally, I preferred getting wet through the rain rather than through sweat. (NB – even if you're walking somewhere cold, you still sweat inside this type of trouser. It's the exercise that's the problem, not the external temperature.)

As a result of their being totally useless for walking in, which is what I'd bought them for, for my first three hundred and twenty-two days of travelling those waterproof trousers saw precisely three hours of use: while tobogganing in the Snowy Mountains, Australia. That definitely wasn't an activity I'd foreseen myself participating in before leaving home – and especially not in Australia – but there we go, that's what happens when you go travelling. The waterproof trousers were of some value on that occasion because I was hopeless at sledging, owing to the fact that I flew off the front of the sledge at the slightest provocation (such as going over a snowflake) and ended up sliding down the hill unaided on my ample backside. The trousers meant that at least I didn't get drenched and cold as well as looking pretty stupid, but I started to question whether it was worth continuing to carry them just on the off chance that I might need to do a bit more tobogganing.

Like the compass, the waterproof trousers did eventually come into their own. This was in South Africa, where I was doing volunteer work which meant I had to participate in twice-daily game drives in open-topped safari buggies – whatever the weather. It rained a lot during those five weeks. The trousers were great at keeping me dry while I was sitting in the lashing rain as we drove around trying to find lions, leopards and elephants. So, they weren't a total waste of space. If you're not planning on doing something similar, though, it might be worth either giving the waterproof trousers a miss altogether and risking the rain, or investing in a proper pair which you'll actually be able to use without effectively boiling yourself in the bag.

Contender #3: the waterproof sarong

Don't get me wrong on this: a sarong is definitely useful. Don't leave home without one. You can sit on it on the beach, use it as a towel, use it as a sheet, even use it as a headscarf in an emergency. Just DO NOT buy a waterproof one. When I bought one, I was told it would usefully be able to double up as a groundsheet. This was neither a good thing, nor was it an accurate thing. The one I had was hopeless as a groundsheet because it was too thin and not sufficiently waterproof to prevent the moisture which was rising up out of the ground from soaking my trousers. In any case, I didn't find myself needing a groundsheet all that often.

What I did find I frequently needed my sarong for was to double up as a towel after showers or after swimming.

Unfortunately, despite not being waterproof enough to do duty as a groundsheet, it was sufficiently waterproof to make using it as a towel disturbingly uncomfortable. Instead of absorbing the water, the waterproofing caused all the drops to run down the inside of the sarong, against my legs, keeping them wet even after they would have naturally dried off. Not a pleasant sensation, especially when the water in question is cold. Which it frequently was. If you can't find a decent sarong before you leave home there are plenty to be bought relatively cheaply in Asia and the Pacific. If you're going the other way round the world, better hope you don't need one before then.

So in conclusion, it's my pleasure to announce the winner of the coveted title 'Most Useless Item in the Backpack'. And the winner is . . . number three: the waterproof sarong.

DOs and DON'Ts of useless items

- DON'T be afraid to get rid of something if you're really not using it and can't see any future use for it. Make space for something else.
- DO take a compass and don't be afraid to use it. Just be careful which set of assumptions your maps are based on.
- DO invest in a decent pair of waterproof trousers if you're going to be doing a lot of walking. Otherwise, unless you're likely to be going on safari in the rain or doing a lot of tobogganing, it might not be worth the effort.
- DON'T be tempted to buy a waterproof sarong. It

might sound like a good idea but trust me when I say it really isn't. Take a normal sarong. Do not, I repeat, do not take a waterproof sarong.

OTHER IMPORTANT THINGS TO DO BEFORE LEAVING HOME

In addition to buying your kit and choosing the clothes and shoes that will accompany you on your journey, there are a few other things you can do before you go to keep yourself looking as good as possible while you're out there enjoying the sun, the men and the extreme sports.

Get your hair cut

Choose a style that will look good and stay in shape regardless of how long it grows, and also a style that doesn't require blow drying, straightening or gallons of products to keep it looking good. If you're getting up at 4.30 a.m. to get a bus to somewhere else you definitely don't want to have to be getting up at 3.30 a.m. to style your hair before you leave. If you're camping you're unlikely to have regular access to electrical sockets to plug in straighteners or hairdryers in any case, and wherever you're staying there may well be times when you'll need to pack in a hurry and won't have time to let them cool down before they need to be in the bag and ready for the off.

If you've got the backpack space take them for special occasions when you've got both the time and the electricity, but don't rely on having them. Also, styling products are heavy so you don't want to be carrying too many of them around. It might not be you to be without straighteners or products, but think of how much good it'll do your hair to have a break for a while. You'll look even more fabulous when you get home.

Get waxed or bleached

You'll have to pack a razor for those times when you need to be in your bikini and you can't get to a salon, but if you've waxed before you go, body hair will take a little bit longer to grow back. Alternatively, if you can stand the long hair and just don't want it to be visible, bleaching might be an option.

Beauty treatments are of course available on the road, so you will be able to keep things neat and tidy if you want to. In South America and Asia treatments tend to be much cheaper than at home, although you might want to just get your legs done the first time you book in with someone new to make sure they're gentle enough to be trusted with more delicate areas. Due to the culture of modesty in Thailand and South-East Asia generally you might find it difficult to maintain a Brazilian there. Remember this is a country so modest that if you get a massage you get it fully clothed (unless you're in Patpong, of course). Your average non-red-light district Thai beauty therapist is not going to be up for waxing your bits. You're going to be shaving it yourself – or possibly getting a very good friend to do it for you. If you're worried about getting an intimate wax abroad or you're not up for shaving, pack some depilatory cream for emergencies.

Put a face on

If you absolutely can't live without make-up, rather than trying to cart a lot of it around with you, consider whether it would be worthwhile having an application of semi-permanent make-up done before you leave home. Certainly if you're fair and cannot exist without mascara, having your eyelashes (and possibly also your eyebrows) tinted will save you a lot of trouble. Mascara doesn't travel well and it hates hot countries.

Get a fake tan

If your first stop is somewhere hot you might want to think about getting a fake tan to avoid being shockingly white through those first few days while you're working on your real one. Remember to take lots of moisturizer to keep your tan looking good for as long as possible, and you might also want to pack a tinted moisturizer for times when your tan has faded just a little bit.

Do a trial pack

All the advice you'll ever read about travelling for long periods of time will tell you to do a trial pack well in advance of leaving home. I read this, I decided I had better things to do with my time, I ignored it. The night before I was due to fly, tears and tantrums attended my packing as it became apparent that there was no way all of the stuff I wanted to take was going to fit into that backpack. Leaving it to the last minute was exactly why I ended up with such a dull, uninspiring and totally un-girlie travelling wardrobe (see page 24). I'd left myself no room for manoeuvre so I had to make quick decisions in a panic. All that achieves is either leaving something vital at home or focusing on the practical to the exclusion of all else. If you don't want to make the same mistake I did and end up feeling like the most unwomanly woman since Attila the Hun, make sure you do your trial pack well in advance of your leaving date.

As you pack things, check them off on your lists. Leave yourself enough time to get to the shops to buy anything you find you've forgotten or replace something with a smaller version of the same if that's what's needed to fit it all in. If it becomes clear that it's not all going to fit, at least you've given yourself some time to reconsider your comfort and coordination priorities and come up with some sensible suggestions as to what to leave behind, instead of flinging things out randomly and screaming like a banshee at any-one who comes to see if you're OK.

If you're struggling to fit it all in, a good tip is to try rolling your clothes rather than folding them. I was really sceptical about this but, surprisingly, it does actually work. Rolled things for some reason do take up less space than folded things. Also, rolling has the added bonus of making everything more easily accessible since it isn't all stacked on top of everything else. Plus, things get a lot less creased than they may otherwise. Having neatly pressed clothes at all times when you're travelling is not going to be your major concern, and most of the time you have literally just wandered in off the street, but it is occasionally nice not to also look like that's the case. Rolled clothes will still crease but nowhere near as much as folded ones do.

A CAUTIONARY TALE

When you first put your backpack together, you might look at it and wonder how you're going to cope when that's all you've got for an entire year. Don't worry, that feeling will soon pass. Despite the fact that you haven't got much in the way of material goods (or maybe because of it), what you do have becomes very dear to you. By the end of the year, you'll be very attached to that dusty, battered backpack and the adventures you've shared.

Imagine, then, my horror on landing in Rio de Janeiro after a horrific three-day flight sequence – which included a night spent at Madrid airport trying to sleep on two chairs pushed together in Starbucks while crying so much because of homesickness that I developed sore patches under my eyes which made me look like a scaly dinosaur – at being told that my luggage had failed to arrive with me.

'The plane was too full at Madrid,' I was told, 'so twenty bags were left off. They'll be sent on the first plane tomorrow morning.'

Annoyed, and wondering why out of two hundred people on the plane my bag had to be one of the twenty left behind, but marginally reassured by the promised next-day arrival, I got a taxi to my hotel and settled in for the night. This was a relatively rapid process, since I didn't have a lot to unpack. My room-mate kindly lent me a T-shirt to sleep in, which was lucky as otherwise things could have got inappropriately intimate, considering we'd only known each other for ten minutes.

My bag hadn't arrived by breakfast but I decided to go out anyway, confident it was winging its way to me. I duly set off sightseeing for the day and returned to the hotel in expectation of being greeted by my luggage. It wasn't there. Things were getting a bit serious now. Not only would there be lots of paperwork involving complex insurance claims, but worse, I was about to start a three-month camping tour and now I had none of the right kit. Having to replace it all in Rio – not the most promising of world shopping destinations, it would have to be said – was not a cheery thought in any case. I was betting they don't have Oswald Bailey in Brazil, and what was I going to do without a head torch? I can think of better places to be required to go on a shopping spree at the insurance company's expense due to your luggage having been lost by an incompetent airline. Milan, maybe? Paris, perhaps? But Rio? Wrong. Yet that was where I was.

To my relief, the luggage did turn up eventually. When I was reunited with my backpack I was so pleased to see it that I hugged both the pack and the somewhat startled driver who'd delivered it. After that episode I got a bit anal about the whole thing and packed more carefully for flights. The moral of this story is that if there's something essential or something you really don't want to lose, make sure it's in your hand luggage. At least then its destiny is in your own control. It's safer to assume an airline will lose your baggage and act accordingly than trust them to get it right.

Plan the fun stuff and the necessary stuff

You'll want to have some kind of leaving do – drinks with your workmates, maybe some form of family farewell and probably an outrageously drunken evening's clubbing with your mates. Get those planned early to avoid stress later and to make sure you can get everyone you want there, there. Then you've got all the more boring but essential stuff to think about, like getting your vaccinations, stocking up on prescriptions, resigning from work, filling in tax forms (if you get the timing right you might get a rebate so it's worth doing), sorting out what you're doing with your car, and getting your travel insurance. Put it all on your lists and work through it in good time. That way you'll be relaxed and looking good at your party rather than being stressed out.

DOs and DON'Ts of pre-trip preparation

- DO address the problem of body hair to make sure you're tidy when you leave.
- DO get a fake tan if your first stop is somewhere hot.
- DO get your hair cut into a manageable style that doesn't need lots of attention or products to keep it looking good.
- DON'T think that you can get away with not doing a trial pack.
- DO remember that rolling clothes takes up less space than folding them. I don't know why this is so, but it is.
- DON'T forget to do the practical stuff in the midst of all the partying.

45

Chapter Two

SLEEPING
WITH STRANGERS

So, you've bought and packed all your kit, been waxed, had a haircut, applied fake tan, partied at all your farewell dos, said goodbye to your mum and got on the plane. Now the adventure starts. Now the world is yours to explore. Now you're officially a backpacker. And, being a backpacker, you're probably on a budget which means you're going to be spending a lot of time staying in hostels. Maybe you're a bit like me – when I set off on my round-the-world trip I'd never stayed in a hostel before. In fact, I'd never backpacked and I'd never travelled on a budget in my life. I had no idea what to expect. To be honest, I didn't give it much thought. After all, staying in hostels is just what you do when you're a backpacker.

If I did think about it at all, however briefly, I didn't really think I'd be spending all that much time in hostels. I figured I'd be busy out and about seeing and doing all the exciting things to see and do in any given destination and therefore all I really needed was a bed and a shower and somewhere to put my stuff. The main difference between hostels and hotels, I reasoned, was having to share your room with a few other people. I'm not that worried about privacy so I didn't think that would be too much of an issue.

I seem to be able to sleep reasonably well, so I wasn't concerned about insomnia and I thought the dormitory thing would be quite a nice way of meeting people. Which it is. In fact, in addition to being cheap, staying in hostels is great as it's an easy way to meet other travellers, swap stories and recommendations, find people to go clubbing with, pick up some work, buy a car, pull, and maybe even find someone new to travel with for a while.

Your guidebooks can offer assistance with finding a hostel that is clean, cheap and in roughly the right area of town but they won't tell you about the little quirks of hostel life which become just one of those things backpackers know about – like how you have to remember to take your room key with you when you go to the toilet. It's definitely worth reading the advice and reports in your guidebooks and in online hostel directories before choosing a place to stay because, like men, all hostels are not created equal. Some have great facilities and are genuinely nice places to stay. Others make you feel like an oversize battery hen. Hopefully you'll end up in the nicer ones but, just in case you don't, here's the good, the bad and the ugly about sleeping with strangers, and how to make it all just a little bit more pleasant.

CHOOSING YOUR HOSTEL

When selecting somewhere to stay, your main considerations are likely to be facilities, location, availability of a bed and, probably most importantly, price. Larger hostels (especially in cities) will often have a travel desk for booking trips and tours, sometimes a bar and probably Internet access (for a fee). They also usually offer the cheapest beds. As a rule, the more beds there are in a room, the cheaper it will be. That's why, if you're on a really tight budget, you can find yourself spending weeks on end sharing rooms with up to fourteen strangers. These larger dorms also tend to be mixed sex. If you're nervous about privacy (or just don't want to share with boys, who can admittedly be quite smelly in an enclosed space), single-sex rooms are available in larger hostels but they're often smaller and so slightly more expensive. Alternatively, you can always stay in a YHA (Youth Hostel Association) hostel as their operating policy is still in the 1950s and they don't generally have any mixed dorms at all. (YHA hostels aren't just a British thing, they're all over the world; in eighty countries in fact, including various European and American locations as well as more exotic places like Egypt, Israel, Japan, Vietnam and Qatar. In most of the rest of the world they're called HI which stands for Hostelling International – but it's all the same organization.)

If you can't get or can't afford a single-sex dorm, you can create yourself a little bit of privacy in a larger dorm by rigging up a small screen around your bed using your towel or your sarong. That washing line you packed unsure whether you'd need it or not might just be handy for that very purpose. Otherwise you'll just have to get changed in the bathroom, under the duvet or tented by your sarong or towel like when you were little and at the beach for the day, trying to struggle out of your wet swimsuit and into some dry clothes without embarrassing yourself.

Large hostel or small hostel?

What you choose depends on what you're looking for. Large hostels tend to attract backpacker tour groups, so can be loud. If you're looking for the party and therefore aren't likely to want to be in bed getting an undisturbed night's rest by 10 p.m., they're often the place to be. The ones with their own bar on site are handy for hooking up with new people and often have cheap drinks on offer, but because they are technically licensed premises they usually have very strict rules about bringing your own alcohol. You're not really supposed to bring it in at all so if you do, don't get caught drinking it. A good tip to avoid detection is to hide it in a soft drink bottle – this works particularly well with things like vodka and coke or gin and tonic but you can get away with white wine as well if you select a soft drink that comes in a green or brown bottle. Red wine and beer can be a little more difficult to disguise though.

The bigger hostels can often also help with things like travel arrangements or luggage storage, and because they tend to be chains, you'll come across lots of them with the same set-up, dotted liberally around whichever country you're travelling in. Large hostels usually have elaborate security systems which mean you'll have to take your room key with you wherever you go – including to the bathroom. Your stuff will be securely locked in your room in these places but you still may not have a locker for it and since people can't be bothered to carry their key around all the time they'll often prop the doors open anyway, so overall the security is probably about the same wherever you're staying. The downside of larger hostels is that they can be a bit impersonal – you're more likely to feel the battery hen syndrome in these, and the kitchens can be a total pain due to lack of equipment and lack of storage space. That's not to say all of them are – some of them have great kitchens.

If on the other hand you're looking for a bit of peace and quiet and don't mind not having an on-site bar, smaller hostels (fewer than twenty beds) might be the answer. They usually have fewer facilities – maybe no satellite TV, maybe only one computer for Internet access instead of fifteen, and you might have to pay a couple of dollars more per night than in the bigger hostels – but the dorms are generally smaller and it can be a bit like living in someone's home, which is comforting if you're feeling a little homesick. It's easy to meet and chat to people in these hostels as well – it's just that there will obviously be fewer of them to meet than in the bigger ones. If you're at all shy, this might be a bit less overwhelming. But don't worry, shyness tends to wear off after you've been travelling for a while anyway.

The people who run these smaller hostels are usually doing so because they genuinely enjoy meeting travellers. They know a lot about the local area and will generally happily help you arrange things to do or see and give you advice about transport as well. If you're a cook, the kitchens are typically less crowded and better equipped than those in larger hostels and occasionally offer extras like salt or herbs which can make a real difference to your meals. Small hostels are individual and like to be different, so sometimes you'll find they sell homemade muffins, or give you a mug of hot soup in the evenings, or sell fresh eggs from the farm down the road. Each hostel is slightly different from the next, which gives you a bit of variety to look forward to.

Deviating from your 'always book the cheapest available bed' rule

If you're seriously on a budget then price is almost always going to be the deciding factor in choosing a hostel. Location is an important but secondary consideration. That said, you don't want to find yourself so far away from the action that you end up spending more on bus or taxi fares than you saved in accommodation costs. The time when location really trumps price is when you have to get up at an ungodly hour of the morning to get some form of transport. At such times, the hostel nearest the departure point should probably secure your booking despite the fact that the hostel a mere fifteen minutes' walk further away is a whole pound cheaper.

When I was travelling, my budget was pretty desperate so I spent most of my time in big dorms in big hostels. There were, however, two occasions during the year when I let myself book something that wasn't the lowest cost option available. The first of these was in Picton, New Zealand, where I was offered a choice of a twenty-eight-bed dorm for NZ$18 a night or a six-bed dorm for NZ$19 a night. I opted for the latter and considered the extra 40p well spent in dramatically reducing the chances of encountering one of the multitude of sleep-interrupting behaviours exhibited by my fellow travellers (of which more later).

The other occasion when I was more than grateful to pay whatever it cost for my accommodation was on the third night of the Inca Trail. This is because at the time I walked the trail there was a landslip between the Sun Gate and Machu Picchu, meaning that instead of walking into the Lost City of the Incas on Day Three, we walked the first two days and most of the third and then descended into the village of Aguas Calientes to leave from there early the following morning. Those three days were tough. As you've probably realized from the episode of the virgin, unmuddied walking boots, I'm not the outdoorsy type and any walks I do in my leisure time at home are the wander-around-in-the-local-woods-in-the-sunshine sort of walks, not the hike up a mountain-in-a-bracing-wind sort.

Day One of the trail was OK. By the time we'd got to the start and gone through all the bureaucracy of getting our passports stamped and permits checked we were only required to walk for a few hours. It was mostly flat, with a short uphill section, a bit of downhill, but nothing too strenuous. I reached camp that night in relatively good spirits. Day Two was a different story. Starting at 6 a.m. after a disturbed night's sleep, the first task of the day was to walk up Dead Woman's Pass. Some of the guys in my group reached the top of the pass within two hours. It took me five. I had become that Dead Woman. As if that weren't enough, next I had to go nearly as far downhill as I'd just gone uphill – and that just to reach the lunch stop. The afternoon held the delights of a second mountain pass to go up and over, and saw me stagger into camp only just beating sunset, several hours behind most of the rest of the group and pathetically grateful that I'd brought flip-flops with me as I couldn't bear to wear my walking boots for a minute longer. The bad news was that it was cold, and it was there, somewhere high in the mountains around Cusco, that I learnt that despite the enormity of the fashion faux pas committed, sometimes wearing socks and sandals is, tragically, a necessary evil. (By the way, in case you ever find yourself in a similar situation, there is an art to wearing flip-flops with socks: you have to pull the toe of your sock out so that it's nice and baggy and then you can force your foot around the post of the flip-flop. It's a common trick used by travellers and campers, but not one I suggest you ever attempt to replicate when back on home soil.)

Having sunk as low as wearing flip-flops with socks, it's difficult to contemplate anything worse, yet Day Three delivered it. Despite the fact that we were going to stay the night in a town, no accommodation was booked for us, as we would have been camping had the landslide not disrupted things. Instead, we were expected to sleep on the tiled floor of a restaurant. No way. Just no way. I winced over the road to a hostel opposite to check their room availability and booked myself into a private room with an ensuite. For the princely sum of £2.60. Never before and probably never again will I spend £2.60 so wisely. It was more than worth it to have a proper bed and a mercifully warm shower after two nights of sleeping on freezing cold ground, walking through the pain barrier and wearing the same clothes for three days straight without washing either the clothes or myself at any point.

What this story is intended to illustrate is that sometimes it's OK not to book the cheapest available option. Don't be too hard on yourself. I know you're on a budget but it's OK to break it sometimes. You'll know when those times are.

CHOOSING YOUR BED

It is possible to find hostels which don't have bunk beds but they're few and far between and should be treasured and appreciated when discovered. Generally, though, sleeping in dorms is going to mean sleeping in a bunk. It's a bit of an adjustment – probably the last time you slept in a bunk bed you were about eight years old? Back then, grabbing the top bunk ahead of your younger sister or brother was cause for celebration. Ten or fifteen years on, the top bunk is an infinitely less attractive proposition. In fact, sleeping with strangers in hostels presents one of the rare occasions in life when nobody wants to go on top.

Which bed is best?

When selecting a bed in a dorm, there are several things to remember. The main one is to try to get a bottom bunk if you can. There are many reasons for this and I'll explain more later. Secondly, consider placement in the room. If you want some degree of privacy, getting the bed directly opposite the door is probably not the best idea, but if you're the kind of person who needs to get up three times a night to go to the loo then the bed nearest the door might be perfect for you. Finally, check out the availability of storage space as you might be able to fit your backpack under some beds but not others, and usually it's preferable to have your belongings to hand, if only to prevent them getting mixed up with other people's. Sometimes you might not have a choice about which bed you end up with if there are already a lot of people in the room, but if that happens, grab what you can and ask around to see if anyone's leaving the next day. If they are, you might be able to move into their spot once they've gone.

A NOTE ON HOSTEL DORM GRAFFITI

It would seem to be a fact of hostel life that wherever there is a wooden-framed bunk bed, there is graffiti. Sometimes, if you're jet-lagged, if it's raining or if you're just trying to pass the time between *Neighbours* and dinner, it can be quite entertaining to read. Clearly you should be proud to rest your weary bones in such a multi-

---

cultural and cosmopolitan sleeping space, previously occupied as it has been by Kurt from Germany, Freddy from Sweden, Sophie from France, Rebekah from Israel, Dave from Australia, Britney from the US and Wim from the Netherlands, all of whom have left you a message the intellectual equivalent of 'I woz ere'. You are also fortunate enough to be able to read the boasts of your preceding bedfellows who seem to feel that the life of all those unfortunate enough to be in subsequent occupation of the same bed could not possibly be considered complete without knowing the details of their predecessors' sexual conquests fulfilled 'in this bed'.

Some of the claims sound quite improbable, some sound like they might be worth a try and others make your fingers itch to write 'Why?' next to them. Into this latter category fell a bed I stayed in in Wanaka, New Zealand, which bore the legend 'I licked a blond guy's arsehole in this bed'. Now why, I ask, whether male, female, straight or gay, would anyone ever voluntarily want to do that? The ponderance of that question kept me busy for quite some time – you see what I mean about the entertainment value.

Reading such fascinating graffiti did occasionally mean that I found myself idly wondering if the 'this bed' referred to meant the top bunk (on which the writing actually appeared) or the bottom bunk upon which these nascent porn stars must have been sat while recording their exploits for posterity. If you're intending to leave similar messages in various locations around the world you might like to think about that question for a bit. And if you are going to leave your mark, please try to come up with something a little more original than 'Shaz and Daz shagged here all night – 15th March 1998'.

Why no-one wants to go on top

So, why is a bottom bunk so good? In itself, a bottom bunk may not appear wildly attractive. After all, you probably haven't slept in a single bed since you moved out of your parents' home. In this case, though, the value of the bottom bunk is comparative, since if you're not in the bottom bunk you must be in the top one, and when it comes to bunk beds, going on top has four key disadvantages.

1. There's usually nowhere to put your stuff. Occasionally a thoughtful hostel owner might provide a shelf at top bunk level, but this is the exception rather than the rule. The problem is that there are some things you need to hand when you're in bed, like your alarm clock, possibly a bottle of water, maybe a book, perhaps your iPod or your phone. All of these things can safely be placed on the floor near to your pillow if you have a bottom bunk. In a top bunk, though, they have to be balanced precariously on the bed, next to your pillow. You sleep uneasily, wondering if they're going to become dislodged in the night and either fall to the floor and break (in the case of your mobile phone or your alarm clock), or fall and hit your bunkmate below. Neither of these is a good outcome. Heavy books are a particular worry. When reading Vikram Seth's *A Suitable Boy* (which is fairly hefty even in paperback) I slept in fear of knocking unconscious a succession of sleeping strangers in bunks underneath mine. Probably not the best way to promote happy intra-dorm relations.

2. You're exposed to the full glare of light in the room.

Bottom bunks are of course partially shaded from this by the less desirable top bunk (or by your towel/sarong screen if you've rigged one up) but if you're in the top bunk when someone comes in to the dorm drunk at 4 a.m. and switches the light on, it has the effect of a floodlight and produces the start-ling and uncomfortable sensation of being rudely awoken by a police raid. And it's a lot more difficult to rig a screen around a top bunk as there's not usually much to attach it to.

3. Getting into a top bunk is not always that easy. The kind of bunk beds you find in hostels are often made of metal. They squeak alarmingly and there's nothing you can do about it. Also, during your climb into bed you have to try to avoid dislodging the precariously balanced alarm clock/book/bottle of water/phone – and that's if you even have access to a ladder. The problem is compounded in those dorms clearly planned by idiots (usually found in the battery hen style of hostel) where the beds are positioned in such a way that the ladders are either jammed up against the wall or sandwiched in by another bed, rendering them completely useless.

In these cases, the available courses of action are a) stand on the lower bunk and haul yourself up; b) jump up and down like a demented grasshopper until gaining enough height to vault onto the bed. The former is not advisable if your bunkmate is already cosied up in their immeasurably more desirable bottom bunk as they will undoubtedly object to receiving your foot in their face. The latter is also an undesirable option, however, as the aforementioned precariously balanced alarm clock/book/phone almost always bounces off the bed as you bounce onto it so you either have to get off to retrieve it and then repeat the whole process all over again, or you have to ask one of the privileged bottom bunk occupiers (who clearly don't sufficiently appreciate their advantageous positioning) to pass it up.

4. In some hostels even if linen is provided (it isn't in all of them), you have to make the bed yourself, which is easier said than done in the case of a top bunk. In this day and age, post the invention of the fitted sheet, it's beyond me why on earth anyone still buys flat sheets. Surely life is too short? But, apparently not. Some people, it would appear, do actually still buy flat sheets and those people own hostels. I don't know about you but I struggle to fit a flat sheet to a normal bed; getting one onto a top bunk requires the contortion skills of a Chinese State Circus acrobat.

How to cope with being on top

To avoid ending up in the top bunk, when everyone bundles off your coach at a hostel, get into the queue at reception quickly, get into the room quickly and have stuff to hand which you can immediately fling on a bottom bunk to claim one before they all get taken up. For those occasions when you can't grab a bottom bunk, here are some survival tips for going on top:

- To minimize the 4 a.m. searchlight effect, invest in an eye mask.
- To keep all your stuff together and not worry about it

62

falling on the floor every time you turn over in your sleep, have a small bag with a long handle to put it all in. Most beds will have some sort of rail that you can loop the handle over to secure it, and you'll know your gear is both safe and to hand. Alternatively, stash things inside your pillowcase.

- If fitting a flat sheet to a top bunk is just too much, either unroll your sleeping bag and sleep on that, or use your sarong as a base.

Dealing with dirty sheets

What to do if the linen doesn't look all that clean? Sometimes you might arrive at a place which supplies bed linen (which, incidentally, is bizarrely known as Manchester in Australia and New Zealand – something to do with Manchester having been the centre of the textile industry, so it's where it all came from when the colonies were set up and it's kind of stuck) and find that the stuff on your bed is not as clean as you'd like it to be. There are a couple of options here. One is to check round any unoccupied beds in the room and, if they have cleaner-looking linen, do a quick swap. The other is to sleep inside your own sleeping bag (which also might not be that clean depending on how long you've been travelling but at least you know it's only you who's made it dirty) or to lay your towel or sarong between you and the sheet or you and the duvet cover so that you don't have to touch whatever it is that you're not happy about lying on.

SLEEP-DISRUPTING BEHAVIOURS
AND HOW TO AVOID THEM

In addition to the practical problems of bunk beds, the other problem with dorms is that sharing a room can, on occasion, be fatal (or at least pretty damaging) to a good night's sleep. This largely depends, of course, on who your dorm mates are. The more people you're sharing with, the more chance you've got of losing on the dorm mate lottery and finding a textbook example of one or more of the classic sleep-disrupting behaviours (SDBs) exhibited in hostels the world over. I know you're going travelling to party and most of the time you think you'll probably have drunk enough not to have to worry about getting to sleep as you'll be at the pass-out-without-taking-your-make-up-off stage, but at some point your budget may give out and you'll have to go to bed reasonably sober. When that night comes, there are quite a few people who might interrupt your rest, but don't worry, here's a guide to the kind of behaviours you might see and a few suggestions for dealing with them or minimizing the impact.

SDB #1: The Snorer
The Snorer is bad news in a dorm. You go to sleep quite happily, then suddenly this noise will start up. Woken from your sleep, slightly confused, perhaps wondering where you are, wondering what's startled you awake and then you

hear it: a noise like a motorbike revving its engine, or like a train, or like a giant pig snorting. It's followed by a keen whistling or irregular heavy breathing which would be the envy of a nuisance caller. Once The Snorer has woken you up, they'll keep you awake because the astonishing variety of sounds they produce is neither routine nor repetitive so you can't tune it out.

The best thing to do with The Snorer is avoid them in the first place if you can. If you're travelling in a group with a known Snorer, try to ensure you're in a different room from them. If you can't do that or you don't know the people you're sharing with, then you need to be equipped to deal with The Snorer. The best tool I came up with for this was in the unlikely shape of the flip-flop; have one to hand to fling across the room at the worst offenders. It's a bit like giving them a poke to make them turn over without actually having to get out of bed. Rubber flip-flops seem to be particularly useful for this purpose as they tend to bounce back and they're not likely to take anyone's eye out if your aim isn't that great. Of course, earplugs can also be of assistance in minimizing the impact of the snoring, but they're sometimes not all that comfortable – and I always worry that wearing them will mean that I miss something I need to hear, like my alarm clock. But if you get on with them then they're definitely a defence against SDB #1.

SDB #2: The Drunken Reveller

This is the person who comes in plastered at 4 a.m. and tries to get undressed and into bed as quietly as possible to avoid waking everyone else up. The problem is that on their way in The Drunken Reveller has created their own personal version of the Blackpool illuminations by switching on every light in the room, so everyone else is awake by now anyway. The Drunken Reveller is a difficult creature to avoid due to its unpredictability. A dorm mate can be a perfect gentleman one night, a staggering, drunken revelling wreck the next. The tool required to deal with this one is an eye mask, as this at least reduces the shock of having the lights suddenly switched on. Screening your bed with your towel or sarong can also help. Alternatively, if you can learn to sleep with the lights on, sometimes it's just easier to leave them on in the first place.

A lesser known but more disturbing species of The Drunken Reveller is The Inebriated Man Who Mistakes the Dorm Floor for the Urinal. Fortunately he is a rare creature but regrettably does make the occasional appearance. You've no doubt heard stories of men who when they're drunk pee in the wardrobe or in a drawer or somewhere equally inappropriate. Perhaps you've even had the misfortune to be in a relationship with one of this breed. If you get one in a dorm, there's not a whole lot you can do about it, except make sure every night before you go to sleep that your stuff is safely stashed under your bed or in a locker and therefore out of harm's way. That and perhaps ask to move rooms in the morning.

SDB #3: The Amorous Couple

If there is a couple in the dorm who are going to try something either a) when they think everyone else is asleep, or b) who are so drunk they don't care whether everyone is asleep or not, or c) who are exhibitionists, the law of averages dictates that they will be occupying the bunk with the squeakiest springs. It's usually the noise which alerts you to this type of activity – that or the bed shaking if you happen to be unfortunate enough to be in the other half of their particular set of bunk beds. The trick for dealing with The Amorous Couple depends on what turns you on.

If you think it's gross, try to ignore them. It's a bit like when you've drunk so much that you know the room is going to start spinning and you have to try really hard to go to sleep before the spinning starts and pretend that a) you're not at all worried about the fact that the room is about to start spinning, and b) even if it does, it's not going to make you feel at all sick. Apply these same principles in attempting to ignore The Amorous Couple. Basically, try really hard to go to sleep, try not to think about what might be going on and try not to listen to the sighs and the moans and the squelches of bodily fluids. Often, the anticipation is worse than the actual event. Lying there with your eyes shut trying really hard not to think about what The Amorous Couple are doing inevitably just makes you imagine quite vividly what they might be doing. This is probably worse than what they actually are doing and if you get to that stage it might be easier just to open your eyes, lie back, think of England and wait till they've finished before trying to get back to sleep. Just pray they're not into tantric or you might be waiting a very long time.

Alternatively, if you're brave enough and you want to stop The Amorous Couple in their tracks (or should that be ruts . . .), you could try getting up, making a lot of noise, going out of the dorm, pretending to go to the bathroom and then coming back in again. If the Amorous Couple in question are not exhibitionists, the knowledge that someone else in the room is awake might make them either stop or leave your dorm in search of an alternative venue.

If, on the other hand, you think the idea of listening to The Amorous Couple might actually be quite exciting then you might want to watch from the start. I know guys who'll admit to enjoying listening to other people shagging; maybe that does it for you as well. It's not for me as, apart from anything else, it reminds me that I'm not getting any. But if a free localized porn show turns you on, then, hey, whatever floats your boat. Just try not to shout encouragement as things build to a climax.

SDB #4: The Plastic Bag Rustler

Of all the antisocial dorm activities, perhaps surprisingly, the hardest one to ignore is The Plastic Bag Rustler. Until you have had the very special experience of sharing a dorm with one of these you might think that the gentle noise of crinkling carrier bags would be unobtrusive. It's not. It's actually so insidious that once you've been woken up by it, it's entirely impossible to sleep again until The Plastic Bag Rustler has finished rummaging through their mountain of bags and located that all important hiking sock which is evidently so critical to their survival at 2 a.m. that they cannot possibly go to sleep without first ensuring that they still have it in their possession. Similarly, the person getting up to catch their 5 a.m. flight who's packing their every possession into carrier bags will keep everyone else awake until he's finished. The only thing that will protect you from this infuriating creature is some earplugs.

DOs and DON'Ts for successfully sleeping with strangers

- DO remember that this is a case where it might be more fun not to be on top.
- DO accept that bunk beds will quickly become the norm for the first time since you were five years old.
- DO arm yourself with an eye mask and some earplugs and don't hesitate to use them, especially if you're a light sleeper.
- DON'T pack your stuff in plastic bags. Rustling plastic bags in a dorm when other people are sleeping is the best way to ensure that everyone else in the room will hate you. And yes, before you ask, they really will hate you even more than the guy who just peed on the floor.
- DO try really hard not to think about what The Amorous Couple are doing in the bunk opposite. I know it's easier said than done, but try. Or alternatively, adopt the voyeur's perspective on the issue and sit back and enjoy. (NB – If you're tempted to be one half of an Amorous Couple yourself, have some

consideration for your dorm mates and maybe use the shower block or the disabled toilet as an alternative venue for your activities.)

- DO break your budget room policy occasionally to save your sanity and get you a hot shower, a comfortable bed and a bit of privacy when you need it most.
- DON'T even think about graffiti-ing the bunk bed unless you've got something really interesting to say.

THE LENGTHS YOU JUST MIGHT GO TO SOLELY TO GET YOUR OWN ROOM

With all this potential for interrupted sleep and the lack of privacy, it's highly likely that, at some point in your travels, you'll no longer be able to stand the thought of another night in the company of fourteen strangers. When you get there, book yourself into a single room for a night or two to regain your sanity. Given that you're on a budget, it may seem an unnecessary extravagance. Trust me on this when I say it isn't. Take some time out and you'll feel refreshed and able to face dorms again. A couple of nights' hit on your budget is worth it as you just don't know the lengths you'll go to to get your own room otherwise. Panicking about my budget, I reached dorm saturation point and went beyond, and here's what happened to me as a result.

In the early stages of my trip, after forty-nine nights of nothing but constant hostel occupation, I was more than desperate to escape. My disenchantment with hostels was concerning as I was just seven weeks into a fifty-four-week trip and I was already completely hacked off with one of the major elements of the backpacker lifestyle. I was wondering whether I could carry on and thinking about jacking it all in to fly home to my own bed, in my own room, with my own duvet. In desperation the solution, I decided – clearly not thinking straight – was to enrol in a scheme where you go and stay with people who provide you with food and accommodation in exchange for your labour. In my case, this meant going to live in an 'intentional community' (yes, it was all a bit hippy) just outside of Auckland and giving up four hours of each day to perform manual labour in exchange for my bed and board. The critically important feature of this decision was not the cost saving (although that was a consideration) but the fact that it got me a single bed, in a single room, all by myself – for a whole week. Me – a suits and offices, dinner parties and doing lunches kind of girl – engaged in re-woodchipping paths, painting walls and digging borders solely in order to secure my own room for a week. Let this be a lesson to you – this is what can happen if you don't give in to the craving for some personal space occasionally.

Should you wish to investigate this option for yourself, it's called wwoofing. It stands for Willing Workers on Organic Farms and operates in around thirty different countries including in Europe, Australia and New Zealand, the USA and Canada. As well as some space and some home-cooked food, you also get to meet the locals and you might just learn something as well. A lot of it is gardening, but my wwoofing has also included making chocolate and cheese, stripping wallpaper and painting.

Chapter Three

FOOD, GLORIOUS FOOD

Even though you'll be busy having the adventure of your life and doing lots of new things, there are still three normal, everyday things you'll have to do, well, every day: eat, sleep and use the loo. We've talked about the sleeping and I'll be getting into the Ladies in the not too distant future, but now's the time to talk about food.

When you're travelling, you'll find that food very quickly takes on a role of epic proportions in your life. It's one of those backpacker facts that you will spend a lot of time thinking about, talking about, and possibly even dreaming about food. Many a long mile spent on buses or trains will be filled with discussions around what local food is good and bad; who's gone the longest without a decent meal; what sort of food you most miss from home; and, critically, what is your dream first meal to be eaten once back on home turf.

Sometimes food is something to look forward to if you're not having such a good day. Sometimes a particular food will make you feel so much better if you're ill or homesick. Sometimes if you're bored and hungry it's just an interesting thing to talk about. Occasionally you might be so eagerly anticipating your next meal that instead of paying attention as a huge chunk of ice falls off a glacier in front of your eyes, or appreciating the colours of a glorious sunset over a volcano, or enjoying the warmth of the sun and the sound of the waves lapping at the most gorgeous white sand beach, you'll be thinking about when the next mealtime is and what's going to be on your plate. It's not ideal, you do need to try to be in the moment, but if Che Guevara, one of the greatest adventurers of them all, does the same, then what have we got to feel guilty for? In *The Motorcycle Diaries*, Che reflects that sometimes when you travel you spend time thinking about amazing things, sorting your life out in your head, and finding the solution to the world's great questions, and other times all you'll really be wanting, so badly that you can't think about anything else, is a bowl of tomato soup. He's right though. It's a cliché but sometimes you really don't know what you've got until it's gone, and your favourite foods are one of those things. Some foods you'll know you're going to miss before you even leave home, but you'll also probably find out that there's some food that you didn't even know you liked that much until you can't have it any more. Mine was chip shop chips – I wonder what yours will be?

EATING IN

Backpacking on a budget probably means that you're going to have to spend a fair bit of time cooking for yourself, sometimes just because it's cheaper and sometimes because there won't be any other choice. If you're camping in the Australian outback the nearest pub is likely to be about two hundred kilometres away and you won't have seen a fish and chip shop since the coast, approximately four days ago. It's cook for yourself or starve. Even when you've got easy access to places to eat out, buying three meals a day in some countries is likely to kick a serious hole in your budget. Unless you're doing the trip on your lottery winnings, eating in is going to be part of the deal.

The places where you're most likely to be cooking for yourself on cost grounds are fortunately also those places where supermarkets and what they stock will be in English and look at least vaguely familiar: places like Australia, New Zealand, South Africa, the US and Canada. Once you've got over the slight Antipodean weirdness of doing your food shopping in Woolworths, it's all fine. If, on the other hand, you're cooking for yourself because you're in a no choice situation (for example, camping in the middle of nowhere) it might be a bit more of a gamble. Places like South America and Africa do have supermarkets, but not quite as we know them. Zimbabwe was particularly challenging – aisle after aisle of large bottles of 'syrup' so brightly coloured it looked radioactive, no cheese at all and a meat counter that was about the size of a small armchair and sold exclusively goat. It did, however, have bread, so it was toast for breakfast, toast for lunch and eating out in the evening so the hunter/gatherer thing was someone else's problem.

Foreign shopping in a foreign language

The challenges of shopping in foreign supermarkets aren't limited to unfamiliar brand names and foreign labelling. Always allow plenty of time for food shopping in non-English speaking countries as it might take a while. In China, you're unlikely to have any idea at all what anything is as nothing will look remotely familiar. My advice – stick with the two-minute noodles and you'll be safe. If you decide to be more adventurous than that, on your head be it. In South America simply choosing fruit and veg was as complex as trying to pick your outfit for the work Christmas party, because nothing looks quite the same as at home. I frequently played the cucumber/courgette roulette since the two looked absolutely identical, and if you think raw courgette on a salad doesn't sound that good wait till you've tried limp, cooked cucumber. On one occasion four of us spent twenty minutes searching for tomatoes, only to find they were in a metre-high pile right in front of us. We'd been ignoring them because they were predominantly yellow and green and a cursory glance registered them as apples. The unavailability of certain critical ingredients can also be an issue causing the premature death of many a promising dinner idea. On the other hand, some foods that you like may be more easily available or cheaper than they are at home because they're locally produced. Seafood is an example of this in certain countries, and if you're a pumpkin fan, you'll love Australia and New Zealand.

Take a phrase book with you when you go food shopping. Even though, quite annoyingly, phrase books always seem to have a section on shopping and a section on food, but never a section on food shopping, if things like cheese and ham are often sold by weight instead of coming pre-packed you need to be able to ask for them in the quantities you want. Watch out for fresh produce as well – another trap for the unwary foreign shopper. Sometimes it has to be weighed and priced in the greengrocery section, not at the till. The best time to find that out is in the fruit and veg section, not, as I did, by being shouted at in increasingly loud and aggressive Spanish after having loaded an incredibly full trolley onto the conveyor belt at the head of a long queue of impatient natives.

Tactics for cooking in hostel kitchens

After you've survived the shopping trip, next up is the murky world of hostel kitchens. The good news is that hostels in countries where finances dictate that you're eating in generally do have kitchens. The not such good news is that the quality of such kitchens and how well stocked they are with equipment is highly variable. Guidebooks may not be too much help as unfortunately they don't tend to tell you a lot about the relative merits of hostels in terms of their kitchen facilities. They do sometimes note the really terrible ones though. But basically, some hostels have fantastic kitchens – spacious, clean, well equipped, and with lots of storage space – and others don't – their kitchens are tiny, overcrowded, lacking equipment and have nowhere to put anything.

In the not so good kitchens, highly specialized skills are required to produce a decent meal. In a tiny and over-crowded space in which fifteen people are vying for the only three saucepans – all of which already need washing up – cooking dinner becomes a small-scale battle of international warfare. With a combination of guerrilla tactics and precise timing, it is possible to outmanoeuvre your opponents and be victorious, so if you find yourself in that kind of kitchen, here's what you need to know:

Tactic #1: safe food storage. It is a strange fact of life in hostels that if you accidentally leave your iPod or credit card on your bed, in most cases it will still be there when you get back. But, on the other hand, people will nick your food. Camouflage is the key to avoiding the kitchen thief; make your supplies as inconspicuous as possible. This works because if no one else notices your food then they can't decide that it looks much more appetizing than their own and steal it. To achieve this, try to choose storage space away from eye level (so go for either the very top shelf or the very bottom shelf) as food thieves are lazy – they'll go for whatever is easiest to get. Store food in opaque bags rather than boxes (which you can easily see into) and tie the bags up. This won't stop a determined thief but it will deter the casual browser.

Tactic #2: avoidance of enemy fridge cleaning agents. The second threat to your supplies is these over-zealous enemy agents who will instantly destroy anything that's not clearly labelled with name, room number and date of departure. It's a bit like being back at school when you had to have your name sewn into everything including each individual sock. If you can't be bothered to stick labels on every single item you have – and let's face it, life really is too short – make sure it's all in a bag and write on the bag instead. Always slightly exaggerate your date of departure to prevent last-minute destruction between the time you check out of your room and the time you actually leave the hostel.

Tactic #3: securing required equipment. In kitchens where supply of equipment fails to meet demand, adopt thorough reconnaissance tactics and use the intelligence gathered to follow these up with a decisive invading move. On arrival in the kitchen, immediately assess the situation and locate the desired equipment. You may need to wash up after someone else, but that'll give you the strategic advantage as no one else will want to wash anything up and will instead wait until someone else has done it. Secure possession immediately (refer to Tactic #4 below) and keep it – if equipment is left unattended, enemy forces will take prisoners while your back is turned.

Tactic #4: occupying required territory. Once equipment is secured and clean, fill saucepans with sauce, pasta or similar to denote occupation and deter equipment thieves. Clearly mark the boundaries of required worktop territory using chopping boards or food bags. Use the filled saucepans to hold hob space. In smaller kitchens, securing and holding sufficient hob space is particularly critical.

Tactic #5: timing of assault. The busiest time for the kitchen is usually between 1800 hours and 2000 hours. To avoid or minimize the need for engagement with others, consider undercover operations in which cooking and eating are performed outside of these hours. Early morning and late at night are ideal. Intelligence gathering can also greatly assist in planning the optimum timing for your assault. Find out the cleaning rota and then use the kitchen in the hour immediately after cleaning, when usable equipment is more readily available and required territory is cleaner and more pleasant to occupy.

The main reason why hostel kitchens can be a little grim is because people don't clean up after themselves. You can't change that; just grin and bear it and try not to let it get to you. In an attempt to force backpackers to keep kitchens clean, hostels the world over have devised elaborate systems. Sometimes it's a bit like being in the army; be prepared to be issued with crockery and cutlery along with your room key and expected to return all items clean and intact before you get your key deposit back. Some hostels take this to the extreme, like the one I stayed at in Perth, Western Australia. Their kitchen contained absolutely no equipment at all. Instead, I was required to decide what equipment I would need in advance, request it at reception and be issued it in return for my room key. I could only have my ransomed room key returned once I'd given everything back clean and dry. If you end up somewhere like this, I hope you're more successful at it than me. I was incapable of thinking in advance of every single thing I'd need so I'd end up traipsing backwards and forwards between kitchen and reception, asking for a strainer or a cheese grater or a vegetable peeler, causing untold chaos in their booking in and out system as well as repeatedly disturbing the bored-looking receptionist's nap.

Portability

Cooking for one when you're on the move on an almost daily basis presents a certain challenge. You have to think quite carefully about what you buy as it has to be reasonably portable. So, you need to have packets and containers that will re-close to avoid spillages (or you need to invest in some small storage tubs) and you don't want to be buying things in large quantities as they're heavy to cart around with you. Most things that have to be kept in the fridge are ruled out because your food has to be able to survive long periods of time between hostels when you can't keep it cold. You might think that eggs are pretty much no go – carrying those around in a backpack could be asking for trouble, because while raw eggs might be good for your hair they're not good squashed on your sleeping bag. If you really want an egg or two for breakfast, though, you can always hard boil the rest and have them for lunch or use them in salads or sandwich fillings. Hard-boiled eggs are so much more transportable. If there's more than one of you, or if you can share the cost and cooking of a meal with others in the hostel, then you'll be able to have a bit more variety. Alternatively, try trading with other travellers if you've got more of something than you can reasonably use.

Pasta, rice and bread will probably become the staples of your travelling diet because they're cheap, relatively nonperishable and easy to carry around. Jars of sauce are also likely to feature quite heavily along with vast quantities of cheap cheese, which does admittedly become rubbery after sitting in a carrier bag on a hot bus for eight hours but, if melted into or over a meal, is still not absolutely inedible. Meat isn't a good idea unless you can buy it in a small enough quantity to use up in one go or unless you're going to be in one place for several nights and don't mind eating a succession of variations on a theme (pasta with chicken, chicken fajitas, chicken risotto). Think of it as a little bit like being back at uni: no decent kitchen and very little money to spend on food because what you spend on food you can't spend on beer.

COOKING FOR OTHERS

As well as cooking for yourself, there might be times when you're required to cook for a group. This happens a lot on budget overland tours as, unlike luxury tours, they don't include a cook as part of the package. Don't expect too much. You're most likely not familiar with mass catering and neither will your fellow travellers be. On the positive side, in situations like this the torture is usually rostered so you only have to cook maybe one day in four. If you're camping, mass catering for the uninitiated becomes even more fun as you've then got gas bottles and limited options to contend with – no ovens on a camp site. Time for more creativity with pasta and rice, and quite a lot of instant mashed potato. If you're looking for ideas, think simple dishes like spaghetti Bolognese, corned beef hash, chilli or stew. You can put pretty much anything in a stew.

There are also some foods that should not be attempted. Kebabs seem like an easy option – but don't underestimate the amount of time required to put together upwards of sixty kebabs. It stops being fun after about fifteen. And don't, I repeat don't, pick macaroni cheese. Trying to stir cheese sauce for thirty is like trying to stir concrete. You end up with blisters in the palm of your hand and I'm sure you can live without joining me as a member of the elite group of People Who Have Actually Injured Themselves in the Course of Making a Pasta Dish.

Shopping on a budget

When shopping on a budget, remember that foods which are locally produced will be a lot cheaper than imports. Another good tip is to look out for whatever is on special offer – you might be able to base a meal around it to give you a break from the usual staples of spaghetti Bolognese or variations on the pasta and tomato sauce theme. The good news is that even on a budget you can still eat relatively healthily if you want to by choosing locally grown fruit and vegetables rather than what you might normally have at home. Look out for reduced price items and if prepackaged quantities in supermarkets are too big, shop at markets instead where you can buy things singly. Go along late in the day to grab an extra special bargain as stallholders sell off leftover produce at knock-down prices.

Ideas for tasty, easy-to-cook and comforting backpacker food

- **Tomato soup** – it's the ultimate comfort food. Combine it with bread and it'll fill you up.
- **Mashed potato** – another comfort food, which is cheap and easy to make. Have sausages with it for a nostalgic childhood treat.
- **Risotto** – one of my favourites. The basic ingredients (rice and a stock cube) are easy to carry around and then you can add to it whatever you like in whatever combination – meat, cheese, vegetables. To make it extra creamy, stir through a knob of butter just as it finishes cooking.
- **Spaghetti carbonara** – simply onion, bacon, pasta and eggs. Cook the bacon and onion in a pan and boil up the pasta separately, then mix them together. Beat the egg (one whole egg and one extra yolk per person), take the pan off the heat and stir through the egg mixture, letting the heat from the pan cook the egg without scrambling it. If you can get it right, it's creamy and gorgeous.
- **Scrambled egg on toast** – to vary it add bacon, ham, herbs, cheese or tomato.
- **Fajitas** – they're a good fun food which you can pack with veg if you want to. If you can't get proper salsa (or it's too expensive), cheat and make it from a tomato-based pasta sauce with the addition of a bit of chilli powder or paprika.

- **Pizza** – buy the bases and make up your favourite toppings.
- **Jacket potatoes** with tuna mayonnaise, egg mayonnaise, cheese or beans – healthy as well as tasty.
- **Yoghurt with fresh local fruit** – a tasty breakfast and healthy too, so you can feel virtuous.
- **Avocado or hummus on toast** – more comfort food; fantastic and relatively healthy.
- **Ratatouille or roasted vegetables** – healthy, tasty and you can vary the ingredients based on what's on special offer, in season or simply available. Also good to use up veg that might be a little bit past its best as it doesn't matter if it's a bit squashy.
- **Soup** – if it's full of veg it'll be healthy and filling, especially if you have a bit of bread to dunk.

Food you might miss

Should you take food with you? If there's something you particularly like and it's something that won't go off quickly, I'd say yes, definitely. Some things you won't be able to get elsewhere in the world or, if you can, they don't taste the same. I didn't realize how much I would miss certain things, so I didn't take anything with me. Mistake. Common things other travellers made me jealous with were tea, chocolate, tomato ketchup and Marmite, none of which taste quite the same abroad. Even when the brand name is the same, the taste is quite different. Occasionally you might be able to find the English version through a specialist food importer, but it'll be expensive.

Now, a word about Marmite. It's BIG on the backpacker scene, dominating many a food-based conversation. Quite apart from anything else, the great Marmite/Vegemite debate is doomed to be eternally unresolved between the English and the Australians and to generate almost as much competitive spirit as the Ashes series. Being English, I come down very firmly on the side of Marmite. And so should you, even if you don't like it. It's a matter of national pride. I suspect that our Antipodean friends who mistakenly insist that Vegemite is better than Marmite are confused by the fact that their supermarkets do sell a product called Marmite (with a red label) – but it's an impostor, a lookalike instead of the real thing. If you're a Marmite lover, don't be fooled into buying the Australian version. It's just not nice. Take it with you instead. Even if you're not a Marmite lover, pack a tactical pot and use it as a bargaining chip in hostel kitchen negotiations. You'll be amazed what people will trade for a taste. It'll be more than worth the investment.

Something else to take with you is little packets of salt and pepper. A bit of seasoning can make an amazing difference to a meal – and again, it's something you notice more in its absence. Things like tomatoes, avocado on toast or fried eggs just taste five times better with a teeny weeny little pinch of salt. Some smaller hostels provide salt, pepper and herbs for your use but most don't. So, stock up on the little sachets they give you on planes, but also pay a visit to your local pub before you leave home – one of those where the cutlery and condiments are self-serve – and pick up a few packets of salt and pepper. While you're there, you might as well grab some mayonnaise, tomato ketchup and vinegar as well. Especially vinegar. Apparently only the English have vinegar on chips. If you're lucky you might get it in Australia or New Zealand, but other than that, the only place in seventeen countries I found proper malt vinegar was in an English pub in Shanghai. And chips taste sooooo much better with vinegar than without.

You might find that what you're craving differs, depending on where in the world you are. In India, for example, almost every second backpacker I met was at the point of active salivation at the mere mention of bacon sandwiches. You can't get bacon in India because half the population doesn't eat pork for religious reasons and the other half thinks pigs are unclean so won't eat them anyway. Malaysia gets round this problem by offering 'beef bacon' instead. As the name suggests, it's beef, cut and smoked to make it taste like bacon. Except that it doesn't quite work. I wouldn't recommend it.

MY MOST MISSED FOODS FROM HOME

Number one on my list was Marmite. Breakfast in a café in Cusco, Peru, which served not only Marmite on toast but also PG Tips and Heinz Baked Beans became a daily pilgrimage for me during my stay in the town. By the time I'd been away from home for a year, I was so desperate for a taste of Marmite that I begged my mum to bring one of my childhood favourites (Dairylea and Marmite sandwiches) to the airport with her to meet me. This was my dream homecoming meal; much discussed and even more anticipated. Other people wanted roasts; I was desperate for a Marmite sandwich.

Coming a very close second in the 'missed food from home' stakes was blue cheese. It was a bit easier to get hold of than Marmite but, outside of Australia and New Zealand, still rare enough to be exciting if found. Very few places in the world have the variety of cheese available that Europe does and in Asia there's hardly any cheese of any sort, especially not blue. Imagine how chuffed I was when I found a block of blue cheese in a supermarket in Xi'an, China, by which point I hadn't had any for at least eight weeks. To the bewilderment and disbelief of those sharing my carriage I ate it on a train, minutes after buying it, without the benefit of any form of cutlery, biscuits or other civilized accompaniment. I still remember now how good that blue cheese tasted.

Then of course there were the chip shop chips. With vinegar. Not something I crave at home, but surprisingly missed when I'm away. Fries are just not the same.

You will spend an inordinate amount of time thinking and talking about food. It's just one of those ways that backpackers enjoy torturing themselves. If you've got slightly masochistic tendencies, you'll love the pleasure/pain combination of imagining and discussing your favourite foods at the same time as knowing you can't have them. That's why tracking down a much missed foodstuff in an entirely unexpected location is a brilliant experience. I'd even go so far as to describe it as orgasmic. And like sex, it's even better after you've gone without for a while. So, if you've been missing out, you've had a bad couple of days, or you're feeling a little lonely or a bit homesick, stretch your budget slightly and cook yourself something really good. It's cheaper than going on a shopping spree and is just as good at making the world look like a better place.

DOs and DON'Ts for eating in

- DON'T underestimate how much importance food will take on in your life while you're travelling. Sometimes it really is better than sex.
- DO take Marmite or tea or ketchup or whatever else with you if you're a big fan. Keep it for special occasions if you like, but at least you'll have it when you really want it. And, believe me, at some point you will really want it.
- DO approach hostel kitchen cooking with military precision. Carefully considered tactics and timing are the key to trauma-free meal production.
- DO trade with other backpackers to get more interesting and varied meals.
- DON'T assume that tomatoes will always be red.
- DO stock up on sachets of salt, pepper and vinegar before leaving home.
- DO your duty to your country and support Marmite.
- DON'T get talked into making cheese sauce for thirty people.
- DO treat yourself to something special occasionally.

91

EATING OUT

One of the great things about travelling is getting to experience different foods and different tastes. Even cuisines you've tried at home don't taste the same when you eat them in their homeland. For example, Chinese in China is very different from Chinese in England. But what is travelling about if not experiencing new things? And even though you're on a budget, the good news is that you will be able to eat out sometimes because there are parts of the world where eating out is so cheap that it's just not worth running the gauntlet of strange supermarkets and hostel kitchens. To find slightly cheaper deals, go to cafés and restaurants just one street back from the main street, look out for set menus and go for local food. Not only will it be cheaper, there's also less chance of you getting ill because the local chefs know how to cook the local food properly but they may not know how to cook Western food properly or, more importantly, how to store unfamiliar Western ingredients correctly.

As with foreign supermarket shopping, phrase books are handy when eating out. They usually have a section on what you might see on a menu, and it's quite nice to know what you're ordering even if you can't pronounce it. Judicious use of the phrase book can also help you avoid the kind of embarrassment my friend Pam suffered when she ordered '*Pie de limón con havaianas, por favor*' from a rather surprised Peruvian waiter. She genuinely had no clue that she'd just ordered a slice of lemon meringue pie with flip-flops, the correct word for ice cream in fact being *helados*, not *havaianes*.

As the experience of eating out varies wildly from country to country, I thought I'd give you a rundown of some of my more unusual experiences so you've got some idea what to expect.

South America

The contrast between the different countries of this region in terms of food is amazing. In Brazil, fresh fruit and veg seems hard to come by and coffee is terrible, which is a bit odd given that they produce it, but I can only assume they export all the good stuff. Cross the border into Argentina, and fruit juice is suddenly plentiful and coffee dramatically improves. While you're there, indulge in steaks and red wine which are both fantastic as well as cheap, and definitely don't miss the local snack food, the empanada. It's a little pocket of pastry filled with some sort of savoury filling (mince, egg and olive traditionally, although now also available with fillings like ham and cheese or sweetcorn with white sauce). Sometimes described as a mini pasty, which is quite misleading, they're extremely moreish. You won't want to wave goodbye to the empanada at the border.

In Chile you could be forgiven for assuming that the national food is the hot dog, so ubiquitous is it. And that's about as good as it gets. In Bolivia and Peru, you can eat very well on a set-price *menú turistico* – usually at least two courses and a drink for less than the price of a can of soft drink back home. There's loads of fruit and veg so you can feel healthy, and freshly squeezed juices are a speciality. You can buy almost every fruit under the sun pulped in a glass. And yes, they definitely are fresh – after you place your order, you'll usually see the proprietor exit the café and run down the road to the nearest market to purchase the fruit in question. Less impressive are the dessert menus, which are a trap for the unwary, having a tendency to promise much and deliver little. Make a working assumption that no matter how many mouth-watering desserts are listed, only about 10 per cent will ever be available and one of these will always be ice cream.

All over South America, but particularly in Bolivia and Peru, you might struggle to pay your bill in smaller cafés and restaurants as small change is in very high demand and most places won't be able to change big notes. If that's all you've got, be prepared for a long wait as the owner runs up and down the road, exchanging the note with other shop-keepers for ever smaller denominations until eventually he comes back with something roughly resembling the right change.

Thailand

This is one of the few countries in the world where street food, even in Bangkok, is safe to eat, is cheap and tastes good. Restaurants are also generally very good value and have menus in English plus waiters who apparently also speak English. Beware though – they know the menu off by heart but absolutely nothing else. Order anything you like as long you want it exactly as it is presented on the menu. Any attempt to change the ingredients, asking for one more or one less topping on your pizza or trying to get your starter brought at the same time as the main course results in a polite smile and nod and the polite but total blanking of your request.

Thai food is good, but forgive yourself if you break the always-eat-local-food rule occasionally. After spending three days in hill tribe villages on a diet of rice, rice and more rice, the return to anything that remotely resembled civilization sent me in the direction of Pizza Hut at the speed of a heat-seeking missile. It wasn't the same as home but I just couldn't face any more rice.

China

Unless you're prepared to eat in five-star hotels and pay five-star prices, you might find Chinese dining experiences to be more of a gastronomic lucky dip than an educated taste selection as it's rare to find a restaurant with a menu in English. If you're lucky, you'll find one with pictures on the menu so you can at least make a semi-informed guess as to what you might be eating. If not, the best course of action is to take a walk around the restaurant, check out what other people are eating, find something that looks vaguely edible and then take the waitress over to that table to point at it. That's a tactic that works anywhere in the world. After you've placed your order, your next challenge is eating it. Again, unless you're in the top-end hotels or over-priced tourist restaurants it's chopsticks or nothing. If you can't already use chopsticks, don't worry. You'll learn fast if you're hungry enough.

If you're in Hong Kong rather than mainland China, you won't have any of these problems. There you'll find the full range of international food options, side by side with the more unusual aspects of Chinese cuisine. Even if you're not planning on eating it yourself, do take a walk down Bird's Nest and Ginseng Street on Hong Kong island. It would seem that the natives do actually eat enough of these items to merit at least ten separate shops selling just these two things. Dried Seafood Road is also a unique visual and olfactory experience, as are the night markets selling roasted scorpion on a stick. Both of these are probably things you should see once in a lifetime but maybe that's enough. Give thanks that you're not a bloke and therefore don't have to try anything and everything, the more disgusting the better, just so that no one questions your sexuality.

India

India, especially northern India, will require a strong sense of adventure, an iron stomach and the ability to be very flexible about what you might want to eat. Your guidebooks will probably advise you to turn vegetarian for the duration. If you're reluctant, just pay a visit to the local market where you'll see butchers' stalls standing proudly in the full heat of the midday sun, selling piles of meat covered in flies arranged next to piles of burning manure. Apparently it's supposed to keep the flies away. It doesn't work on the flies but it'll probably work on you.

Curry is, of course, the order of the day. You'll be given it literally each and every mealtime. Unless you've got a particularly strong stomach, after about seven days you'll be ill. Maybe it's something you've actually eaten or maybe it's just the fact that your stomach's hacked off with having been fed curry three times a day for a whole week. If you're in India in the first place, you've probably got sufficient sense of adventure to cope. You just have to accept that you're going to be ill at some point and if you manage to escape without having had an upset stomach then you can count yourself extremely lucky indeed. If you do get ill, India is virtually guaranteed to provide you with a really good toilet story – I'll be coming on to the importance of those later.

So, already you're eating nothing but vegetarian curry and you can't get bacon for love nor money. Visit a town like Pushkar, site of a sacred lake and the holiest city in Rajasthan, and you'll find that religious reasons mean that meat, fish and eggs are completely banned along with any form of alcohol. This is something to take into consideration when planning your itinerary. Do you want to be stuck for three days in a town where there's not a whole lot to do and you can't even have a decent night out?

As if that's not enough, your stomach will also find itself dictated to by the country's constantly fluctuating electricity supply. You can go into a café, order toasted sandwiches (which are almost as good as tomato soup as a comfort food), and then be told a few minutes later that they're off the menu as there's no electricity. So, you'll make your second choice and then the waiter will reappear with a wide smile to say that the electricity supply has been restored and would you still like the toasted sandwiches? My record was a lunch order that changed four times in twenty minutes. Do let me know if you can beat that. Some places even cater for the likelihood of power failure. I found a restaurant in Varanasi which actually had two menus; one for the daytime and the other for the evening. Everything on the evening menu could be cooked over an open fire because even though the power is erratic all day, the supply is reliably non-existent in the evening.

Local specialities

At some point you will expend significant amounts of time and energy hunting down the food you miss from home with the focus of a hundred-metre sprinter leading the race with only two metres to go, but the rest of the time you'll have lots of opportunities to try new things. In most cases the best advice is to suck it and see. If you don't like it, order something else. Some of the stranger things I've eaten in my time are: llama and alpaca (on a Bolivian pizza), eland biltong (South Africa), kangaroo (Australia), camel and crocodile (Nairobi) and barbecued crickets (Thailand). OK, so the crickets were a dare, but they weren't too bad. Crunchy and, somewhat disappointingly, exactly like eating barbecue flavour crisps. Llama, alpaca and kangaroo are pretty good, crocodile was a touch bland, I think eland's an acquired taste although generally biltong is pretty good, but camel's tough and leaves a remarkably unpleasant aftertaste in the mouth. Probably should have seen that one coming. Just in case you're wondering, by the way, biltong is a South African speciality – meat that's seasoned with salt, pepper and herbs and sun dried. Proper biltong is moist, not at all leathery, and it's good. Try some if you're there.

I will admit I lost my bottle over the Peruvian national dish of guinea pig. Definitely not a meal for the faint-hearted. Served whole, it's complete with head, feet, eyes, ribcage, organs and brain – the only thing missing is the skin. You can be forgiven for passing on that one. You might also want to give the Australian classic of a pie in a bowl of mushy peas a miss. Apparently lots of English travellers do. My guess is that the reason for this has quite a lot to do with its name. I don't know about you but I reckon it's pretty difficult to seriously consider eating something called a 'floater'.

Chocolate

A word about chocolate. It's clearly hugely important. For some of us, there are certain times of the month when easy access to chocolate means the difference between being a balanced, happy person and the female version of the Incredible Hulk. If this is you, then I'd definitely advise that you take an emergency stash with you, as the brand names exist the world over but what's inside the wrapper is not the same. Sometimes it's fun to check it out, though. You'll enjoy Australia and New Zealand, which have an amazing variety of Cadbury's chocolate, most of which you can't get in the UK. My personal favourites are New

Zealand's Black Forest (containing bits of chocolate flavour biscuit and pieces of cherry jelly) and Australia's Peppermint (which is milk chocolate with a green fondant mint centre). Weeks of amusement available for sampling all the different flavours to see which ones you like.

Cadbury's in India is a different proposition altogether. I'm not sure if it's the milk they use (which is probably goat) but Indian chocolate is dry and dusty. Melt in your mouth it does not. Try it once if you will, but I challenge you to go there again. American chocolate is equally strange in taste and texture in a way which, frankly, defies description. Vomit comes close, but even that doesn't quite get there. South African chocolate is worth a go. One note of caution: in hot countries be very careful about how and where you pack chocolate. After six hours in a hot bus it's going to be more liquid than solid and while it would make a fab body paint by that point in time, it's not so good smeared all over your camera. If you can, wrap it in a plastic bag so if it does turn liquid it's at least contained, and try to keep it flat so it doesn't ooze out of shape too much. If you're carrying food that's been in the fridge, put the chocolate in with that to help it stay cooler longer.

DOs and DON'Ts for eating out

- DO be prepared to try new things.
- DO look for set deals and special menus.
- DO try to eat local food.
- DON'T feel bad if you don't want to sample everything new.

100

- DON'T assume that just because a dish is on a Bolivian dessert menu it will actually be available any time that week.
- DON'T worry about having to use chopsticks – you'll learn fast if you have to.
- DO take chocolate with you from home if it's critical to your emotional well-being.
- DON'T feel bad about the fact that it is possible to be put off eating something just because of its name.

Chapter Four

KEEPING SPICK AND SPAN

Matters of hygiene and cleanliness – always close to a girl's heart – are probably a faintly terrifying prospect for those of you about to go overseas for the first time. At home, in the comfort of your own bathroom, you've got good mirrors, good lighting and all your favourite lotions, potions and creams. Best of all, you know who uses it and you know it's clean. There's no getting away from the fact that when you're backpacking, you'll most likely be sharing bathrooms, using a variety of public toilets, and you may not be able to wash your clothes as often as you would at home. You will probably get a little bit out of your comfort zone when it comes to cleanliness but never fear, there are ways and means to make yourself feel a bit better about things. I'll share with you my coping strategies and top tips. I learnt the hard way so you won't have to.

WASHING YOURSELF

If you're in hotels, even budget ones, your bathroom will probably be OK. It might not be too tastefully decorated (think 1970s brown) but it'll be serviceable and at least you'll be the only one using it. If you're in hostels or you're camping, though, the chances are that you're going to be sharing a bathroom and that it might not be as well equipped or as clean as you'd like. To a certain extent, you're going to have to go with the flow. Here's how.

Top tips on using shared bathrooms

Do a recce of the washroom facilities and the toilets fairly early on after arriving at a new place. That way you're prepared, and won't be trying to cope with something you're not entirely impressed by at the same time as being desperate for the loo. It'll save you multiple trips back to your room as well if you know what you need to take with you and what you don't. For example, is there space to change in there and somewhere dry to leave your clothes while you're showering? If not, you might be better off getting undressed in your dorm (or your tent) and doing a short towel-wrapped dash to the shower. Better that than a pile of soaking wet clothes to deal with – unless you lose your towel on the way, of course. To save your blushes, make sure you've got it tucked in tightly.

Coping with dirty shower stalls is easy – make sure you wear your rubber flip-flops into the bathroom and keep them on while you shower. They'll separate you from the goo on the floor and they'll dry off pretty quickly afterwards. Also, if you're short-sighted (like me), then this is one situation where you have an added advantage over people with good eyesight – and that's not something you can say every day. If you simply don't wear your glasses or lenses into the shower in the first place, you can't see the gunk on the floor and it seems so much easier to deal with then.

Surviving cold showers

Learning not to scream when the shower is cold is easier than you might think. No, it isn't particularly fab to get up at 5 a.m., trek across the campsite and then find there's no hot water, but it'll certainly wake you up and shock you out of that hangover pretty sharpish. And a cold shower is great for getting your circulation going, will instantly deflate eye bags, shrink pores and leave you with a fantastic rosy glow to your skin.

The best way to have a cold shower without suffering immediate heart failure is to stand slightly out of the water and run your hands through the shower in a sort of continual rolling/flapping motion. This splashes the water onto you and gets you used to the temperature without having to put your whole body under it straight away. The aim is to splash yourself with the water, and once you've got yourself sufficiently splashed to be able to lather up, just wash yourself off one bit at a time.

Washing your hair in cold water is, let's face it, fairly grim, but it will make it shiny. If cold water is all that's available to you, believe me, you really can benefit from my experience.

I spent eight months of my trip torturing myself to an unnecessary degree with cold showers. I don't know about you, but cold water cascading down my back is somehow both worse and seemingly colder than the same water anywhere else on my body. I'd stand under cold showers, desperately arching my back away from the water while at the same time trying to keep my head under it in order to rinse out the shampoo. It wasn't until Month Nine on the road that I suddenly realized that it was much easier, much more comfortable and far less distressing to face the shower, bend from the waist and hang my head into the water. That way, the cold water only got on my hair, not on the rest of me. For a supposedly intelligent woman, I'm still at a loss to understand how it took me so long to figure that out.

In addition to shiny hair and improved circulation, cold showers also make you really appreciate hot ones, so each time you arrive at new accommodation you can enjoy that moment of excitement, hope and anticipation when you find out whether you've now got a hot shower.

A WORD OF WARNING ABOUT SOUTH AMERICAN SHOWERS

After several cold showers, you'll probably be unreasonably excited at the prospect of a hot one, but be a little cautious if your hot one turns up when in South America. With flagrant disregard for health and safety, South American hotels, campsites and hostels frequently choose to heat their water by the effective, if somewhat alarming, route of passing an electric current through a shower head. It does heat the water, but it also means that if you touch the shower head at all, you're likely to get a fairly sizeable electric shock. Since you're standing in water at the time, that shock is amplified. Also, since South Americans are generally of fairly small stature, the shower heads tend to be set quite low, increasing your chances of banging your head on them. This is an instance when taking a shower could literally kill you. However, you should have an insulating material in your backpack – one that will prevent an electric current from earthing through your body. Yes, this is yet another occasion when it's absolutely essential to WEAR RUBBER FLIP-FLOPS.

Bucket showers

Bucket showers are an interesting variation on the more conventional form of plumbing, which you may come across if travelling through South-East Asia, particularly in the more rural areas of Thailand. Frankly, the term 'bucket shower' is a little grandiose. 'Bucket' would in fact be far more accurate.

If presented with a bucket (or similar large-ish container) of water and what looks like a ladle, the procedure is simple:

1. Undress and stand within easy reach of said bucket.
2. Use ladle to scoop out some water.
3. Throw water all over yourself.
4. Repeat as necessary.

At first this might seem a bit weird but it's a great opportunity to relax and enjoy yourself. After all, the last time you were allowed to throw water all over the floor without your mum telling you off was probably when you were about three. Here, there's no one to tell you off, you're not going to have to clean it up and you can make as much mess as you like. Go on, make it playtime, release that inner child!

A NOTE ABOUT TRAVEL TOWELS

During my pre-departure kit-purchasing frenzy, I was persuaded to buy myself some travel towels. These beasts are allegedly super-absorbent, quick-drying and fold up really, really small. They did indeed do exactly what it said on the tin; they dried very quickly and they took up very little space in the backpack. A double-edged sword, though, was their super-absorbency. Apart from having the descriptive disadvantage of making them sound like a sanitary towel, this had to be a good thing, didn't it? Wrong. Super-absorbency is a very good thing when drying yourself. It's not so good when you accidentally drop your towel into one of the grey, gunky shower tray puddles. Within seconds it had sucked up something like three times its own body weight in disgustingly dirty water. Don't try this at home.

Despite their super-absorbency, drying yourself with a travel towel does take a certain amount of practice. You wouldn't think using a towel would be a challenging activity, but believe me, there's a technique to this one. Basically, travel towels resemble nothing so much as a large chamois leather. If you rub your skin as you would do with a normal towel, a travel towel simply redistributes the water around your body. Instead, you have to wrap each body part tightly in the towel and wait for it to whisk away all the water before moving the towel onto the next area to be dried.

Be patient.

It is worth it because the alternative is a conventional towel which will take ages to dry, so ultimately you'll end up packing it away while it's still wet, making your backpack smell like a damp dog.

What to do with your valuables

Showering with your valuables is one of those strange experiences that only happens to backpackers. It's also an experience that is predominantly the preserve of solo travellers. If you're in a hostel with no lockers and you're a bit paranoid about your stuff like I am then you probably won't want to leave your passport, money, credit cards, camera and iPod lying on your bunk when you head off to the showers. Which means you either have to leave it with someone else or you have to take it to the bathroom with you. Which then means you have to find somewhere to put it when you get there. I spent a year trying to precariously balance all my important stuff in a stack on the floors of various bathrooms or suspend it all from inadequately sized hooks on the backs of various shower doors AND try to ensure it wouldn't get wet. Just before I was due to fly home I realized I should have bought one of those small dry bags that you use to put your camera in when you go out on boat trips to save it getting splashed.

A word about baths

Baths are not a common commodity in the backpacking world, unless of course you're hotelling it. Hostels and campsites generally don't have them as they'd take up too much space and encourage you to use too much water. For me this wasn't too much of a hardship as I'm the kind of person who only has a bath if I've got a spare three hours, a good book and a bottle of wine. If you like a bath, though, you might want to consider booking yourself into a hotel occasionally to try to ensure you get one.

When you have no access to a bathroom

What to do if you have no cleaning facilities? If you've got hair so oily you could fry chips for a small village with it, you can put dry shampoo or talc near the roots, rub it in to soak up the grease, then brush it out. Not something to be done on a day when you want to wear a dark top, obviously. Alternatively, you can scrape your hair away from your face with a hairband, which will instantly make you look more fresh-faced. Or if all else fails, either put on a hat or cover it up with a bandana. For the rest of you, wet wipes are the answer – particularly useful on a trek.

DOs and DON'Ts of keeping yourself clean

* DO recce hostel and campsite bathrooms before you need to use them so you know what to expect.
* DO wear rubber flip-flops into the shower – both to avoid stepping in the gunk on the floor and to prevent

death by electric shock.

- DON'T force yourself to stand under a cold shower – splash it on instead.
- DO be extremely careful if using any shower head with electric wires running into it.
- DO enjoy the opportunity to be a child again and throw water all over the place with absolute abandon.
- DON'T lose your patience with your travel towel – just wrap it tightly round you and wait.
- DO consider purchasing a small dry bag for your valuables, particularly if you're travelling alone.
- DON'T expect to find a bath very often. If you do like to have a bath, plan some time out specially for it.

THE BEST SHOWER OF THE YEAR

Two showers were particularly memorable for me. The first was the hot shower I had after completing the Inca Trail. It wasn't a particularly special bathroom or a particularly fantastic shower, it was just the fact that after walking for three days in the same clothes and only having been able to have a cursory wipe with a Wet One during that time I smelt pretty bad. Fortunately everyone around me was in the same situation so no one noticed how bad each other actually smelt, but nevertheless being able to stand under running water and feel clean again was the most amazing feeling. Almost orgasmic.

The second most amazing shower was purely a matter of location, location, location. A stay in the Mariepskop mountains of South Africa provided the year's most scenic shower. Heating the water in the wood-burning 'donkey' beforehand took an age but it was more than worth the wait. To stand naked, a gentle breeze caressing my skin, soaping myself down while enjoying the uninterrupted view of a glorious sunset over the lush valley below, and knowing that no one could see me, was quite simply a small piece of heaven.

WASHING YOUR CLOTHES

Keeping your clothes clean while you're travelling is likely to be a bit more of a challenge than it is at home, and you might have to live with washing them less often than you'd ideally like to. Try to adopt the attitude early on that in most cases, if your clothes are a little bit dirty, it doesn't actually matter so long as they don't smell. This is especially the case if you're in some remote rural location when trekking or doing any sort of trip which involves you taking only a limited amount of clothing. After all, who is going to see you anyway? Pretty much the only people you're going to meet are other travellers and they're likely to be in the same state as you are.

You may want to try to keep at least one outfit 'for best', as it were. This will mean that you'll always have something reasonably decent to go out in. I reserved a dressy top and a skirt (together with the sparkly flip-flops) as my evening 'going out' clothes and also tried to keep a pair of jeans reasonably tidy for occasions when I wanted to look smartish but didn't want to overdress by wearing the skirt.

The options for keeping your clothes clean while you're on the road are several. You can:

- Hand wash them yourself.
- Use washing machines in hostel laundry rooms.
- Pay for hotel laundry services.
- Use laundrettes and washing services.

Hand washing

Hand washing isn't all that much fun, is it? While you're in another country, you're probably going to have better things to do than slave over a bowl of wet clothing. But it's a useful option when you're about to run out of underwear as you can rinse it through and leave it to dry overnight.

You will need to invest in two items in order to successfully hand wash. The first is some concentrated travel wash – it's smaller, lighter and easier to lug about than a carton of washing powder and can double up as shower gel or shampoo if you get really desperate. The second critical item (which I made the mistake of leaving off my packing list and had to rectify quickly once I was on the road) is a universal plug. Very few campsites and hostels have sinks with plugs, and it's very difficult trying to wash clothes in running water – not to mention the amount of water you waste. My research shows that a pair of balled-up knickers is not an effective alternative.

Hostel laundries

Hostel laundries, where they exist (which tends in the main to be the more developed countries like Australia and New Zealand), are generally well equipped with both washers and dryers. Your biggest challenge is going to be finding the correct change to operate them with, but once you've achieved that, just load your stuff in and off you go. Reception will often have small sachets of washing powder available to buy so don't bother trying to carry around a big heavy box of the stuff – it'll be a pain and it'll leak everywhere.

For some bizarre reason there always seem to be fewer driers than washers in these places. Try to ensure that you're available to hang around the laundry room when your washing is due to finish (allow about forty minutes as a general rule) and you'll find that you can often jump the queue for the drier. If someone's stuff has finished and they're not there, just take it out, leave it in a reasonably neat pile on the side and replace it with your own.

Remember that some things you won't be able to tumble dry. The major one is your travel towel. Don't think it'll be OK to tumble dry it once or twice because it won't. It simply won't work effectively once you've done that. It'll be like trying to dry yourself with the cover of a hardback book. Jeans are another one – they'll shrink. For anything that can't be tumble dried, there's often a drying room available for you to hang stuff up in but I would sound a note of caution here. Things left in drying rooms often go missing, so if possible it might be better to take things back to your dorm and try to hang them there. Make sure you don't hang wet washing over someone else's bed or backpack, though. You won't be popular if you make someone else's dry stuff wet.

Laundry services

Using laundrettes or laundry services requires less effort on your part but does introduce the necessity for forward planning into the laundry process. Using laundry services inevitably involves leaving the laundry overnight and therefore can only be done on days when an early departure is not planned for the following morning, as you have to be able to wait until the laundry is open to collect your washing. Many were the times I found myself with only three remaining clean pairs of knickers and at least five days until my schedule offered a window of laundry opportunity. In that situation, you're either going to have to resort to hand washing a few pairs, or the other good standby is to wear your bikini bottoms instead. Before handing your laundry in to your hotel or hostel check the costs, as they often charge by item so can be quite expensive, whereas external laundries tend to charge by weight.

Generally in places like South America, Thailand and India, laundry services are quite cheap (in the region of 50p for a kilo of washing) and they are less hassle for you. Your guidebooks will be able to point you in the direction of good places to go. Submitting laundry to washing services in developing countries, however, can be something of a roulette game, so develop a sense of adventure about these things. Sometimes the washing takes longer to be done than originally promised. I had a few anxious moments wondering whether my washing would be ready to depart before I had to and on one occasion I had a fascinating trip around the flat roofs of neighbouring buildings somewhat voyeuristically shuffling through piles of other people's underwear in order to find my own. If that does happen to you, you can always just insist, politely but firmly, that they give your laundry back to you as you need to leave. You might then have to dry it yourself but that's better than losing half of your already limited wardrobe.

Avoiding laundry mix-ups

Washing identification is an interesting science. In order to avoid the potential for embarrassing laundry mix-ups, some laundry services operate a method of sewing a small length of coloured thread into each and every single item of clothing; a different colour for each different customer. So, don't be surprised if your freshly laundered and pressed clothes return with tiny coloured tails. They take a while to unpick but it's best to do so to avoid untold chaos and confusion at future laundrettes. I'm pretty sure that getting the wrong knickers back from the laundry is not what you meant when you told your friends that your round-the-world trip would hopefully offer a few opportunities to get into someone else's pants.

The coloured threads were a bit annoying but the most bizarre method of identification I came across was the South American laundry who stapled small paper tags into the laundry. Yes, I did say stapled. What??? I really didn't get that. For one thing, surely the paper was at risk of disintegrating in the wash; for another, did they really think they'd pick up much repeat business? Cursing and breaking my nails while trying to extract staples from my underwear was painful enough, but that was nothing to the uncomfortable day ahead if I missed one. I did have a small smile to myself, though, at the evident confusion I'd caused the stapler (the person, not the actual instrument used) when deciding where exactly to attach the tag to one of the few luxury items I'd allowed myself to pack: a lacy G-string.

The great advantage of using laundry services rather than doing it yourself, especially where they're cheap, is that the clothes do come back pressed as well as washed. It's one of life's simple pleasures to put on clean, fresh clothes. It's one of those things that you take for granted at home but once you've been backpacking for a while it really makes a difference. Enjoy it.

A NOTE ABOUT GETTING YOUR WASHING DONE IN INDIA – AND HOW TO HAVE SIN-FREE UNDERWEAR

Firstly, Indian laundry marking is different to the rest of the world. They sew in something that resembles a luggage tag of brown cloth marked with strange symbols. I was assured that the tags (known as dhobi marks) merely identified where I was staying, although it looked to me more like an obscure occult practice than directions to my hotel.

Secondly, in most countries laundries operate behind

closed doors so you can't witness the agonies to which your clothes are being submitted. As with so much else, India – a country where concepts of privacy are somewhat different from our own – was an entirely different prospect. I'd hand my laundry in at the hotel reception in the morning, then in the afternoon I'd be taking a stroll around the local town and would see my clothes being beaten black and blue on sloping stones in the local river. In a process fatal to any buttons, washerfolk would thrash the clothes around in the river, dump them on a large stone, rub vigorously to remove stains, slap the clothes about a bit and then wring them to within an inch of their life. The moral of this story is: don't take anything you actually like to an Indian laundry as it may never be the same again.

If you visit Varanasi, you'll have the opportunity of a lifetime: to have sin-free underwear. Now, that's not something you get every day, is it? The Ganges at Varanasi is considered holy, and most Hindus make a pilgrimage there at least once in their lifetime to bathe, as bathing in it is said to cleanse you of all sin. The local laundries similarly use the Ganges to wash your underwear, so by my reckoning that must mean it's sin-free too. For a few days at least.

DOs and DON'Ts for washing your clothes

- DO use laundry services where they're available – it'll help the local economy, give you more time for sightseeing and fun stuff and means you get your clothes back ironed and smelling fresh.
- DON'T submit delicate or treasured items of clothing

to laundry services as they may not be the same again – especially in India.

- DO invest in some concentrated travel wash and a universal plug as you will need to do some hand washing at some point.

- DON'T be tempted to tumble dry things that can't be tumble dried. You haven't got that much stuff with you, so you don't want to ruin what you have got – but also be careful of leaving anything desirable in drying rooms. Keep the good stuff in your dorm.

- DO plan ahead with your washing – there's nothing worse than running out of clean knickers. Remember if you do run short, you've always got your bikini bottoms as a standby.

- DO approach laundry, as with everything else when you're travelling, as part of the adventure. Relax, compromise a bit and don't worry too much about clothes that don't smell.

USING THE LOO

There's not really a nice way to put this, is there? We're girls, and we'd rather not think about it. Unfortunately, though, it's one of life's essential activities so I'm sorry, I'm just going to have to talk about it.

Personally, since I'm not into water sports and I have a curiously un-British dislike of toilet humour, it's not often that I find myself discussing the finer points of bathroom behaviour. Such matters are, however, one of the staples of backpacker conversation. Once you've been travelling for a while, you will find yourself openly chatting about the state of the toilets in whatever locality you happen to be in at the time. You will also find yourself sharing intimate details of your bowel movements and world toilet experiences over dinner with fellow travellers whose names you either can't remember or haven't even been told in the first place. Don't panic – it will become normal. I promise. It's another one of those things where you just have to relax and go with the flow.

Making the best use of your guidebooks

Your guidebooks will probably provide some useful info on using the toilet in the particular countries you are visiting. Things they usually cover are:

- Toilet paper carrying requirements – the essential information as to whether it's necessary to have toilet paper about your person at all times, or not. In some parts of the world, not persistently carrying toilet paper with you wherever you go is a serious error of judgement. You just don't want to go there. If in doubt, carry toilet paper. If budgeting is a bit of an issue and you don't want to keep having to buy rolls, stock up from someone else's supply whenever you do happen to find some in a toilet. Hotels, restaurants and cafés are very good for this. In any case, carrying toilet paper or tissues is a useful habit to get into even at home – how many times have you tried to use the loo in a pub or a club and found out too late that there was no paper?

- Toilet operation – you wouldn't think that there were that many possible ways to vary the mechanics of a flushing toilet but designers and engineers the world over seem to have managed an astonishing degree of innovation. Your guidebooks will often give you an indication of what the flush may look like and how to work it. Chains, buttons, levers, handles – there seems to bc a bewildering array of mechanisms. I remember a brief but horrid episode during which I spent five minutes in a desperate hunt round the toilet cubicle getting more and more sweaty and panicky as I realized that, while it might be a tiny room, no I really couldn't find the flush. Just as I was thinking that I was going to have to exit quickly and hope that no one else was waiting to come in behind me, I discovered the flush, which turned out to be an almost invisible foot pedal. On the other hand, the flush might be as sophisticated as a bucket of water and a bowl. The trick with that is to drop the water from a height sufficient to generate appropriate clearing force without being so vigorous that spillage is caused.

- Toilet paper placement – the critical information as to whether to flush the paper or fold and place in the bin next to the toilet. This is crucial – get that one wrong on a busy campsite and your name will be mud when the toilets block and the pervading stench wafts appetizingly over the entire site. Also important to note in preservation of the delicate stomachs of fellow travellers is the fold bit of 'fold and place'.

THE IMPORTANCE OF HAVING A GOOD TOILET STORY

Having a really good (meaning, of course, a really horrifying) toilet story is like a rite of passage amongst backpackers. Along with a battered backpack, sensible shoes and a really good head torch, a tale of truly terrible toilet experience is the unmistakable signature of the serious traveller.

So, when you're enduring that hideous toilet experience, think of the plus side: that's the beginning of your traveller's tale. A bit like the 'one that got away' story that fishermen tell, you're welcome to embroider and colour it a little more each time you tell it.

Squat toilets

Personally, I think that whoever invented squat toilets must have been a sadist or an Olympic level gymnast. With nothing to hold on to, you have to balance yourself at an especially unnatural angle, strain your thigh muscles to the point of agony, attempt to aim straight, all while trying to avoid ducking any body part or item of clothing in the puddles on the floor. Squat toilets on trains are even more of a challenge as then you've got to try to predict and counterbalance the movements of the train – but at least they usually give you a handle to hold on to. Looking on the bright side, squat toilets are actually more hygienic than normal public toilets as you're not sharing a seat.

There are a few tricks you can use to make squat toilets more bearable:

- Secure any loose clothing to avoid the worry of dunking it in puddles on the floor. Tuck skirts into their own waistband and roll trousers up to the knee. Do not wear them if you think there's any possibility of having to use a squat toilet as yards of trailing material and squat toilets do not mix. This is a common problem in Thailand where fisherman's pants are available very cheaply from the markets. If you are caught short in a pair of them, the best option is to remove them completely and put them well out of the way.

- Get your toilet paper out of your pocket well in advance of any squatting manoeuvre. This is much easier than risking disrupting your precarious balance while ferreting around in your trouser pocket when the pocket in question is screwed up somewhere around mid-thigh.

- Finally, and most importantly, it is essential to slather the area above your upper lip with Tiger Balm, as no other odour can possibly compete with the smell of that stuff.

After using squat toilets for a while, you may also find you've developed slightly more respect and understanding for those men who seem incapable of aiming straight. I was previously quite sniffy about little sprinkles left on toilet seats by certain members of the male of the species, but once I discovered that even when hovering over a squat toilet within point blank range of what is admittedly a fair-sized hole it was still possible to miss, I had a little more sympathy for men who fail to hit the target. Although, of course, they have had a lot more practice at it than us.

The correct way to use a squat toilet

This may sound obvious but I was doing it wrong for months. In a squat cubicle, you should face the same way as you would in a normal toilet (i.e. facing the door rather than the rear wall). If you don't, as my Thai guide so accurately put it, 'Somebody's gonna see your ass'.

MY OWN TRAVELLER'S TOILET TALE

I'd been warned by other backpackers that China was the worst place in the world for toilets. My first few days there didn't live up to that – the toilets at my hostel were Western and clean. It was on Day Three of my stay there, however, that I found myself caught a little short while taking a walking tour around the hutongs (traditional alleyways) of old Beijing.

I'd noticed earlier that the city appeared to be amply blessed with public toilets and I found one very quickly.

It was a little whiffy, but with my protective Tiger Balm under my nose, I strolled in confidently. Then very nearly exited again at much higher speed. All that kept me there was the desperation of the situation.

I was faced with a series of squat holes in a row along the wall, each separated from the next by a two-foot tall sheet of metal. There were no doors whatsoever. The horror. Even worse, the first three holes were taken so I had to wander past three curious Chinese to take up my position over the fourth hole. Once there, the desperation which had driven me in there in the first place instantly evaporated and I was faced with an acute case of stage fright, much to the amused curiosity of the Chinese who were all peering over the partition to see what was going on. Nor was this an isolated example. Even in places like the airport and at train stations, privacy was not a consideration. In fact, never mind the doors, I counted myself lucky if there were walls separating the squat holes.

All I can say is thank the gods that I'd been told the correct way to face when using a squat toilet before I got to China.

Bush peeing

If you're backpacking, it's likely that there's going to come a point when you need to bare all, be at one with nature and just let it go. Looking at the positives, bush peeing is generally cleaner and less smelly than using public toilets. It gives you an opportunity for an airing, and let's not forget that sometimes a bush pee can provide the ultimate loo with a view. When you've got to go, you've got to go, so you might as well enjoy the sights.

While the entire world has the potential to be a man's toilet, it's a little more difficult for those of us of the female persuasion. Ladies have certain requirements in this respect, not the least of which is the attempt to preserve some degree of modesty. There is, however, a technique to feminine bush peeing and my trial and error experience has allowed me to perfect the tactics. I therefore humbly offer up the following advice to make bush peeing a bit less traumatic:

- When scouting around for a bush pee site, look both above and below you as well as around, and when you think you've got a suitable place, squat briefly to check the sight lines at that level. Squatting might mean you can see someone or something that you can't see standing up, and you probably don't want to be overlooked. I once had a very traumatic experience when a Quechan goat-herd on a hill above me (who I'd failed to notice when selecting my spot) started waving enthusiastically at me while I was in mid-flow.
- When selecting some undergrowth to provide you with cover, do not choose a thorn bush unless you really have to, and if you do have to, do not under any circumstances back into it. In fact, it's useful to use an exploratory finger to touch test the prickliness of any vegetation you're planning on using as cover before you bare all to it. Your finger is a lot less sensitive than other parts of you.

128

- If in the desert, be very aware of the fact that dry ground is not very absorbent. Watch out for splash-back. If you have a bottle of water with you it might be useful to spill a bit of it on the ground to soften it up a bit before you start.

- Don't make the mistake of positioning yourself at the bottom of a downhill slope. It's quite difficult to simultaneously maintain your precarious balance, pee and jump out of the way of streams of urine racing towards you.

- Rubber flip-flops are this season's (and in fact any season's) essential accessory for bush peeing. The possibility of misdirected aim is the same with the bush pee as when using a squat toilet, so if you do happen to have an unfortunate accident you can simply rinse them off and no one will ever be any the wiser.

If you are really traumatized about the whole bush peeing experience, then try to minimize your chances of having to go by making sure you use the toilet before you leave your accommodation and make use of any stops en route, even if you don't feel the need to go. (Do I sound like your mum?) Also, if cover is a problem, you can ask two friends or travelling companions to turn their backs and hold up a sarong or a towel to provide a screen. If the worst comes to the worst, you can always use your washing line and a towel to rig up a screen.

DOs and DON'Ts for on-the-road toilet trips

- DO go before you start out.
- DO enjoy the view.
- DO remember to test surrounding vegetation for spikiness before finalizing your spot.
- DON'T ever pee at the bottom of a downhill slope.
- DO make a habit of carrying toilet paper with you at all times.
- DON'T worry about talking to absolute strangers about your bowel movements – it's perfectly normal when you're backpacking.
- DO have some sympathy for guys who can't aim straight.
- DON'T be too embarrassed if you do find yourself being forced to use doorless toilets. Probably no one is watching you anyway. Treat it as a backpacker rite of passage and turn it into a good story.

Chapter Five

HEALTH

OK, I admit it – health isn't going to be the first thing you'll be thinking about when you're planning your trip. No doubt you're far more excited about where you're going and what you're going to be doing and, while you're sorting everything out, health might not seem all that important. And no, it's not the most exciting thing about travelling – but it is one of the most important things. If you fall ill, have an accident or end up in hospital, it's going to seriously disrupt your trip. If it's really bad, not only could it get very expensive, but the worst case scenario is that you could end up on a plane home. So, even though it is a bit dull, taking good care of yourself is very important – and that starts while you're still in the planning stages and carries on once you're actually out there, doing it all.

BEFORE YOU GO

There are a few things that you can get organized before you leave home that will help you have a fit, comfortable and healthy trip. It's worth putting the effort in now, instead of paying for it later. Here's what you need to do:

133

Get insured

I'm going to go into Mum mode about this one. Before you set foot on that first plane, you absolutely *must* make sure you have good travel insurance. Not only will your insurance provide a safety net in case your stuff gets stolen and potentially some compensation or assistance if your travel arrangements get stuffed up, but it will also cover the costs of medical treatment, should you need it – and believe me, that gets expensive. You'd need to be Posh Spice to pay your medical bills if you need emergency care after an accident and if you ever need to be airlifted out of anywhere (not an impossible scenario if you break a leg while hiking somewhere hilly and remote) a multi-million lottery win isn't going to cover it. The rest of the world doesn't have the NHS. Countries in the European Union have some sort of reciprocal agreement with the UK, so you might get some treatment there without charge providing you have the appropriate card, available from the Post Office. But anywhere more exotic than that, if there's anything you need done, you'll have to pay for it – whether it's seeing a doctor for your dodgy tummy or getting a broken arm plastered. In some countries, hospitals will not even start treating you until they have a fax from your insurance company guaranteeing that they'll pay for your treatment. All of which means insurance is *the one thing* you cannot afford to be without. Got the message? OK. Mum mode off.

Lots of companies now offer specific backpacker travel insurance which, as well as the usual, also covers some adventure sports and activities. There is a fair bit of choice out there so shop around and compare the deals on offer, rather than just taking the first one presented to you by your travel agent. It'll only take an hour or so of Internet research and, to make sure you've got cover for all the stuff you need cover for, it's an hour well spent. If you think you might want to do lots of adventure activities and dangerous sports, check the small print of the policy so that you know exactly what is and what is not covered, as if you injure yourself doing an activity which isn't covered your insurance won't pay out for any treatment you need as a result. If necessary, you may need to take out extra insurance specifically to cover a particular activity. Don't assume that the company running the activity will be insured and you can claim off their insurance. As illustrated by the case of the South American showers, health and safety standards vary dramatically across the globe and in some countries having adequate insurance cover may not be a pre-requisite of running a business.

Have your jabs

Whether you need any vaccinations or not will depend on where you're travelling to. If they're recommended for somewhere you're going, it's usually worth having them. Yes, even if you hate needles. Just one needle now might mean that you avoid lots of needles later. Just don't look when you're having it done.

To find out what you need, start by booking an appointment with your local GP. There should be someone in the practice who can advise you about what you'll need for which countries. When you go, take with you a list of the places you'll be visiting and, if you can, a detailed itinerary showing exactly which parts of each country you'll be going to. Some health risks apply to certain parts of a country but not others (for example, risks in jungle areas may be different from risks in mountainous areas of the same country).

Some vaccinations are available on the NHS; others you'll have to pay for – either at your doctor's surgery or at a travel clinic. What you might have to pay for depends largely on where you go to get them, but yellow fever is one that is often charged for and that you must have if you're going to certain parts of South America. Rabies is also usually a jab you need to pay for, but you're unlikely to need that unless you're going to be working with wild animals in places like Africa or Asia. Your GP will let you know what you need to have and where you need to go to get it. Sometimes you might need more than one appointment as some vaccinations require more than one jab, and sometimes you have to have different jabs at different times because your body can't handle everything at once. This means it's important to get organized early. Don't go to your GP two weeks before you're due to leave – give it at least a couple of months. If you have to have quite a lot (like I did), your weekly visit to the nurse will start to become part of your routine, quite normal and unremarkable. A word of advice, though: remember that regular injections aren't normal for those around you. Don't send a text to your mate after one of these visits saying, 'OK, I've been stabbed, so I'm on my way now. C u at 7.' They tend to panic.

Don't be tempted to ignore having your jabs – vaccines are not just about prevention from illness (or at least reduction of its effects); for some countries they're part of the entry criteria. If you don't have the certificate to prove that you've had the right jab, you're not coming in. Unfortunately, customs officers are harder to crack than bouncers – flirting with them doesn't change their mind. You really won't be coming in unless you've had the right needle. So, as well as going to your doctor, check the visa and entry requirements for all the places you're visiting to make sure there are no requirements like this waiting to trip you up. Check the immigration websites of the countries you're travelling to for the most up-to-date information.

Stock up on drugs

By which I mean the legal kind, of course: prescription medicines, contraceptives and malaria tablets (if you're going somewhere where you need them). Malaria tablets are complicated things. The quantity and type you require depends on lots of variables like which tablet is best for you, which ones work in the region you're visiting, and how long you'll need to take them for. It's best to ask your GP's advice on this, as some tablets are only available on prescription so pharmacists won't necessarily be able to discuss all the options with you. Budget for these – they can be expensive – but don't be tempted to cut corners here. Malaria is not a pleasant disease and, no matter how careful you are, you're pretty much bound to get bitten at some point.

If you use any prescription medicines on a regular basis, or have prescribed contraceptives, you'll need to talk to your doctor about this well before leaving home. Sometimes it may be possible for your doctor to prescribe enough of it in advance to last the trip, but if not, you'll need to restock on the road. Your GP can advise you as to where might be best to do this, and I've also got some tips on that which I'll share with you later. If you need to carry prescription medicine in your cabin baggage rather than your checked luggage (for example, insulin), you may need a note from your doctor to explain why you need it with you. If you're going to be carrying a large quantity of medication, regardless of how you're packing it, it may also be advisable to ask for a doctor's note to explain what it is and why you're carrying it. This is to avoid potential problems with customs, who may otherwise haul you up as a drug dealer – and I for one don't fancy being told to drop my trousers and bend over for the internal examination.

This advice also goes for contact lens solution, and if you wear glasses, make sure you pack a spare set in case something happens to the ones you wear every day.

Buy a first-aid kit

I mentioned the importance of a first-aid kit when I was talking about what to pack. It's worth the investment – both in cash and packing space. You might only need it once but when you do need it you'll be glad you had it. Don't be scared by the words 'first aid', even if they bring back long-buried and vaguely dreaded memories of practising resuscitation at Girl Guides with a dummy which tasted of antiseptic, or wrapping your friends' arms in slings. When I say take a first-aid kit, I'm not necessarily suggesting that you'll need to perform emergency first aid on yourself or anyone else (although obviously if you do, having a first-aid kit will be handy). Instead, I'm thinking that you might need normal, everyday lotions and potions for things like athlete's foot.

As well as the emergency stuff (just in case), what you really need as a traveller is the kind of stuff your mum has in a tin in the kitchen cupboard. The stuff that you assume is always going to be somewhere around the house. Except that when you're travelling, your mum's kitchen cupboard won't be in your backpack, so having this ordinary, everyday stuff to hand will make your life a whole lot easier when you're not feeling great, since the alternative is trying to buy it, or at least something like it, locally. Trust me, when you've got a cold and feel like snuggling up in a warm bed and telling the world to go away for the day you really don't want to have to drag yourself to a foreign pharmacist and try to mime your way through a shopping list of headache tablets, decongestants and throat sweets.

If you don't want to bother with trying to buy everything you need separately, check out the specially designed travel first-aid kits available in travel stores and pharmacies. Exactly what you need to take with you will largely depend on where you're going and what you're likely to be doing, but you might want to include:

139

- **Antiseptic cream and/or wipes** – to prevent infection if you get a minor cut or scratch.
- **Plasters** – to cover any cuts and keep them clean.
- **Tape and some sort of dressing/bandage** – to cover a wound which needs something bigger than a plaster (hoping you don't need it, but it's better to have it and not need it than need it and not have it).
- **Painkillers of some sort (aspirin, paracetamol, etc.)** – useful for headaches, other pains and, most importantly, for hangovers.
- **Antifungal cream** – to treat infections like athlete's foot, which you could possibly pick up in communal bathrooms or swimming pools and which will be painful if you leave untreated.
- **Calamine lotion** – to soothe and cool bites or rashes, helping you to avoid scratching them and making them worse.
- **Iodine tincture** – which can be used to make water safe for drinking (ensure you follow the instructions on the packaging very carefully).
- **Antihistamine tablets** – for allergies (which you might get somewhere else even if you don't get them at home) but also to reduce itching if you have a lot of insect bites.
- **Antihistamine cream** – to reduce swelling and stinging from insect bites or allergic reactions.
- **Rehydration sachets** – essential if you've suffered from a bout of diarrhoea, but also quite helpful in the event of a bad hangover.

140

- **Throat lozenges** – if you feel rough, these might help you feel a bit more comfortable.
- **Diarrhoea stopping tablets** – to be taken with caution, but helpful in avoiding embarrassment if you get a bout on the day when you have to spend fourteen hours on a coach and don't have easy access to a toilet.
- **Blister treatments** – especially if you're planning on doing some serious walking.
- **Insect repellent** – essential. It's better not to get bitten in the first place than deal with itchy lumps afterwards.
- **Suncream** – another essential. The health risks associated with sunburn are huge (skin cancer being the most obvious) but also because serious sunburn makes you feel like you're on fire inside, will make you miserable and will make you peel and lose that tan you worked so hard on.
- **Decongestant tablets** – like the throat sweets, these'll just make you feel a bit better if you get all bunged up.
- **Moisturizer** – to revive your skin after being in the sun, soothe dryness and help you hold on to your tan. For really dry, cracked skin, something a bit more heavy duty like Vaseline might be good.
- **Lip balm** – to help you remain at your kissable best because sunshine, cold and wind can really dry your lips and when you're travelling you might be spending a lot more time outside than you do normally.
- **Safety pins, tweezers and nail scissors** – because you never know when you'll need to hold something together, pull something out or cut something off.

If you have any allergies at all, make sure that the products you choose are safe for you to use and if you buy a pre-packed first-aid kit which contains something that you're allergic to, remove it before you travel as then there is no risk of you using it by accident.

Some of the travel first-aid kits available include needles and syringes (and a letter of explanation). If your route takes you into developing countries, you might want to invest in one of these so that if you should have to go to a doctor or, even worse, end up in hospital, you can ensure that the equipment used on you is clean and sterile. If you do get one, remember that you won't be able to have it in your hand luggage on planes.

Preparing to cope with periods

They're not much fun at the best of times, are they? (Except for that brief moment of relief each month when it starts and you know for certain, that you're absolutely, definitely, not pregnant.) Sadly, I can't pretend periods are in any way fun when you're travelling either. Squat toilets and bush pee stops don't tend to come with sanitary bins and if you can't flush and you can't bin, you'll either have to bury or bag. If you bag, it needs to be in sealable plastic as you'll be carrying it until you can find a bin. Looking at it that way, maybe the effort required to dig a hole and bury it is worth it. That or try to hang on until you get somewhere slightly more civilized.

When we were talking about packing, I mentioned that some countries just don't do tampons and suggested that if you can't cope without them you should take an adequate stock with you. Alternatively, if packing space is lacking, you could consider some of the other products on the market (such as the Mooncup) that fit internally and can be rinsed and reused. This could be your answer to packing problems, but bear in mind that they do need to be boiled occasionally to sterilize them, which could prove a bit tricky in communal kitchens.

If your periods are particularly heavy or troublesome, or even if you'd just prefer not to be bothered with them too much while you're on the road, you could discuss alternative options with your doctor (such as going on the pill, having a coil fitted or getting a contraceptive implant) – all of which could potentially lighten your menstrual flow. These are obviously more drastic options and, because they interfere with your body and hormones and have potentially longer-term effects, you'd need to discuss in detail with your doctor the possible impacts and possible side effects before you make any decision.

If this is an avenue you'd like to explore, start the process early to give yourself plenty of time to find out about the various options available and come to a decision that's right for you. If you do go for something like this, allow enough time for a reasonable trial period (and I mean months, not weeks) before you leave on your trip. You don't want to have a coil fitted the day before you fly off to Thailand and then find out three days later that it's painful or you've had a bad reaction to it and need to have it removed.

DOs and DON'Ts of getting prepared for a fit and healthy trip

- DO ensure that you've got adequate medical insurance that covers all the activities you want to do and will pick up the tab in the event of an emergency or accident.
- DON'T wait until two days before departure to go to your doctor to find out what vaccines you need.
- DO make sure you either have a stockpile of your prescription medicine before you leave home, or you have a plan for how you're going to get more when you need it.
- DO invest in a first-aid kit – both for emergencies and for everyday health issues, like colds or allergic reactions.
- DON'T take needles or large quantities of prescription medicines with you unless you have doctor's notes explaining what they're for and why you're carrying them.
- DO pack plenty of tampons, or seek advice on alternatives well before you go.
- DON'T tell your mate you've 'just been stabbed' after having your jabs.

ON THE ROAD

Once you're out there, travelling, you're the only one around to look after yourself. As well as being conscious of your personal safety and not putting yourself at risk of being a crime victim, it's just as important to look out for your health. Use your first-aid kit to administer to minor ailments, but if they persist for longer than a couple of days, go and see a doctor – or at least seek the advice of a pharmacist. It might cost you, but it'll be worth it because the alternative is ending up with something serious which costs even more to treat. If you have an accident or get sick, there might not be a lot you can do about it except get medical help, but some things can be avoided and, if you can, avoid them – it'll make your trip much more enjoyable, comfortable and worry free.

So hot, you're not

Avoidance is definitely the best policy when it comes to sunburn. It's unattractive and uncomfortable, so to avoid it wear long, loose clothing and a hat, and also ensure that you're constantly applying and reapplying suncream. If you do want to get a tan, do it gradually – don't sit in the sun for six hours on the first day you find a beach. Remember that the sun in some other countries is a lot hotter and more damaging than in the UK, so even if you don't burn at home, you might well burn when you're abroad.

145

Sunlight reflecting off water will fry you more quickly than usual, so if you're swimming, or out on a boat, be extra careful. To protect your shoulders when swimming wear an old T-shirt over your bikini, and watch out when snorkelling – burning your bum or the backs of your knees is not fun. If you think an old T-shirt will seriously compromise your hot beach babe image, think what bright red and peeling skin will do to it – and that lasts a lot longer. Serious sunburn will also impair your pulling power – you won't be able to do anything interesting with that hot man you picked up in the bar because when your thighs feel like they're on fire you don't want anyone anywhere near them, even if it is the six-foot blond surfer dude who's rumoured to be extremely well endowed.

If you do get burnt, keep the skin well moisturized and covered up until it's had a chance to heal. Badly burnt skin will peel off to reveal new skin underneath which will be ultra sensitive to sun, so even after it's cleared up, take extra care not to be exposed to the sun for too long. Aloe vera or calamine can soothe burning hot skin, so try to find some lotions or creams containing those ingredients to ease the pain, or even the aloe vera plant itself. As well as damaging your skin, sunburn will also dehydrate you so keep drinking plenty of water for a couple of days afterwards. If you get a headache with your sunburn or start to feel sick or dizzy after getting burnt, you should seek medical advice as you may actually have sunstroke.

Remember that you can also get sunburnt when it's not that hot, especially if it's snowy. Sunlight reflects wickedly

off white surfaces, so if you're going skiing, visiting a
glacier or even driving across salt flats, make sure you're
smothered in sunblock and sporting sunglasses. Snow
blindness is as serious as it sounds.

Being bitten

Love bites might be quite fun to get; insect bites aren't.
They're irritating and you won't be at your attractive best
if covered in red, swollen lumps and constantly scratching.
To avoid getting bitten either cover up, so that the pesky
little things can't get to you in the first place, or use insect
repellent. Use it at night as well as during the day, and if
necessary sleep under a mosquito net where possible. Don't
forget to put repellent on your feet (the pulse points there
are strong so they are attractive to mosquitoes), and also try
to avoid wearing perfume as insects love it. You really don't
want to recreate the Lynx effect with a cloud of mosquitoes.

Lavender and citronella are known as natural insect
repellents and smell better than commercial chemical
preparations – although their effects don't tend to last as
long. They're most easily available in essential oils, which
should never be applied directly to the skin, so you'll need
to mix them with a carrier oil before applying them.
Travellers' lore also suggests that vitamin B and garlic repel
insects. Vitamin B is found in Marmite, amongst other
things. Don't worry, you don't have to spread Marmite and
crushed garlic onto your skin; it works through ingestion –
although I have no idea how. I did seem to get more bites
after my Marmite ran out – who'd have thought Marmite

would be medicinal? Alternatively, you could of course simply take vitamin B supplements, and if you don't want to take too many tablets, use strong insect repellent and also suncream containing repellent.

If you do get bitten (which you probably will, no matter how careful you are), try not to scratch. It not only scabs and looks ugly, but can also get infected. I know that's like telling you not to swoon at Brad Pitt, but try. Rub in the cream or dab on the calamine lotion to reduce the itching and take antihistamine tablets if it's really bad. If you've also been sunburnt, the antihistamine should give some relief there too. If any bites get swollen and don't reduce within a day or two, or you start to feel sick or dizzy after being bitten, seek medical advice.

A NEAR-DYSENTERY EXPERIENCE

Despite the horrors of doorless public toilets, you may be surprised to hear that China wasn't the scene of my worst toilet experience. Instead it was India. Through personal experience, I can tell you that it is not for nothing that 'Delhi belly' is one of the nicknames for travellers' diarrhoea. Almost every traveller who goes to India gets it at some point. Maybe it's down to the excess of curries, maybe it's due to a distinct lack of kitchen hygiene, who knows? You won't be worrying about that when it's you who's clutching your stomach and running for the nearest bathroom (or bush), anyway.

My previous experiences of travellers' diarrhoea had been that it hits a couple of times and then goes away again. Not in India. In India, I had to run to the loo every ten minutes, and had serious sweats and waves of cramping pains for a whole nine hours. After about three trips to the loo, that's sore. After twenty-three times you start to wonder if you'll ever be able to sit on a hard chair again. It's grim, but a diarrhoea story like that is, along with the battered backpack and the terrible toilet tale, one of those rights of passage that mark out the seasoned traveller from the novice.

My bout was so bad that my tour leader called a doctor as she thought I might have dysentery. I'll admit that did worry me a bit. I associate dysentery with school history lessons about life in the trenches during the wars. I thought the world had moved on a bit since then, but not India apparently. Maybe it's not surprising that a World War era disease is a possibility in a country in which a guide explaining Hindu funerary customs opened his talk with the words: 'First we purify the floor with cow dung and cow urine. . .'. This is why you need diarrhoea tablets and rehydration sachets with you.

Anyway, as it turned out, I didn't have dysentery. This was established during a three-minute visit from a doctor who prodded my stomach twice, prescribed some expensive and nasty-flavoured tablets, told me I was to eat nothing but rice and lentils for three days and then charged me twenty quid for the privilege. His pronouncement on the matter? I was affected only by (and I quote) 'normal travellers' diarrhoea'. NORMAL????

If you happen to get a bad attack like this which lasts longer than a day or two, seek medical advice in case it is something more serious, take the tablets, drink a lot of water, stay in bed and ponder the only silver lining: that you do lose quite a lot of weight, quite quickly.

Restocking your medicine 'cabinet'

If you need to replace something in your first-aid kit or get more of your prescription medications while you're away, it isn't as difficult as you might think. Take a trip to the local pharmacy to check out what you can buy over the counter and, if you can, take the old packaging with you to show the pharmacist, as even if they don't have exactly the same thing, they may have something else with the same active ingredient. You might also spot some familiar brand names, or even find that you can just buy something that you need a prescription for at home. Thailand is great for this – it has Boots the Chemist. There's definitely one just off the Khao San Road in Bangkok and another one in Chiang Rai. There may be more dotted about the country that I didn't find. Either way, it's extremely reassuring to see the familiar blue sign when you're far from home.

If you can't get what you need from a pharmacy, you'll need to actually visit a doctor. It's obviously going to be easier to do this in an English-speaking country, so if you're going to need to get more of a prescription medicine then plan your itinerary carefully to ensure that you leave home with enough to last you until you get to a country where you can easily restock. I'm guessing the thing most of us will need to get more of en route is contraceptive pills. It's pretty easy in Australia, New Zealand and Canada, where they have family planning clinics similar to ours. A local phone book or a quick Internet search should give you the contact details and address – either phone up or pop in to find out what they can do for you. You may have to pay a registration fee in order to get an appointment and the pills themselves aren't free like they are at home. If you happen to be in Asia when you run out, Thailand is probably going to be your best bet for replenishment. Boots might just have your tablets in stock (you often don't need a prescription) but if not you'll probably be able to find a clinic or a doctor where English is spoken. I wouldn't try this in India or China unless you're really desperate.

SEX ON THE BEACH

It sounds terribly romantic and if you get the chance you might well want to indulge. But sex on the beach isn't without hazards, and I don't just mean ending up with sand in very unfortunate places. Here are some of the things to watch out for:

- Crocodiles – seriously. In parts of Australia it's not safe to go on the beaches because of the man-eating salt-water crocs. Look out for signs, and if there are any, don't do it. You might fancy getting eaten, but presumably not literally.
- Getting caught – not only potentially embarrassing but also illegal in some countries, so could lead to arrest. Two Brits got a prison sentence for this in Dubai – and you wouldn't fancy having to explain that to your mum, would you?
- Your clothes being stolen – risky in poorer countries where clothes are high value, but also consider whether your mates (or his) would do this to you for a laugh – the walk of shame is bad enough without having to do it naked.

- Getting wet (and not in the right way) – watch out for the tides. You might have found a nice secluded cove for your activities but if the tide comes in it won't just be secluded – you'll be stranded.
- Drowning – someone did actually die in Australia while giving a guy a blow job in the sea. The guy got overexcited and was holding her head to his bits so tightly that she couldn't come up for air. Imagine having that on your headstone . . .

Safe sex

I know I keep banging on about this (no pun intended) but it's easy to forget when you're away from home in an exotic location, you've had a couple of drinks, picked up a gorgeous guy, gone for a romantic walk along the beach and are about to get down and dirty in the sand. Pausing the action to ferret around in your bag for a condom may not be your main concern – but it should be. Especially with a partner you don't know. You probably wouldn't trust them with your money, your credit cards or your passport so don't trust them with your health either. The effects of losing that are far more long term.

To minimize the awkwardness of these situations, always make sure you've got a condom or two with you, especially when you're going out in the evening. I know that's a bit like putting decent knickers on (i.e. the kiss of death in terms of seeing any action) but if you need one you'll be gutted if you haven't got one – and, as I said before, in some places the Ladies aren't very well stocked in this sense. It's much better to take your own rather than take the risk. They're only small – just pop a couple in your bag, and a couple in your pockets (if you've got any). Stash one in your bra if you need to – that way he might even find it for himself without you needing to say anything. If you're no good at putting them on, don't stress it, just give it to him. Alternatively, you could try to make it fun. I have a friend who boasts that she can put one on with her mouth – she recommends practising on a cucumber. Maybe you could try to learn that before you leave home. It'd be a good trick, wouldn't it?

And finally, if you're on the beach, DON'T get sand stuck to the condom, it chafes like you wouldn't believe. If you think cold wind makes your lips sore . . .

DOs and DON'Ts of looking after yourself on the road

- DO cover up in the sun – or ensure that you're constantly applying sun cream.
- DON'T forget that water reflects, so take extra special care when swimming or on boats.
- DO remember that as unattractive as you may feel pasty white is, red and peeling is worse – don't overdo the sun exposure in your quest for the perfect tan.
- DO drink plenty of water when you're out in the sun and afterwards. Not only will it help avoid dehydration, it'll also help keep your skin in good condition, which will mean your tan will last longer.
- DO use repellent to keep insects at bay – and if you

want an excuse to eat Marmite, that's as good a one as any.

- DON'T scratch.
- DO be reassured by the presence of Boots in Thailand.
- DON'T be tempted to have sex with a stranger without using a condom. It's just not worth the risk.

Chapter Six
THE SCARY STUFF

The minute you book your trip and start telling people about it, they'll start telling you travel horror stories. You'll also find that suddenly the media is full of stories of Brits abroad being mugged, pickpocketed, robbed, kidnapped, stabbed, raped or even murdered. You'll never have heard so many of these stories before. You know how you buy a car and you think it's a really unusual colour, then the week after you get it you notice that every third car is actually that colour? Well, it's like that. For some reason, your friends and acquaintances delight in sharing the bad news with you. It's like you become the repository for travel horror. You'll become very familiar with these tales. They usually start with, 'Oh, you're going to XYZ place. Do be careful there . . .'. I had such gems as:

'Oh, you're going to La Paz. Do be careful there, that was where we had our wallets stolen by someone pretending to be a policeman.'

And:

'Oh, you're going to Thailand. Do be careful there, that's where my friend had all his clothes and all his money stolen on a beach.'

At least these first-hand stories have some degree of

accuracy about them. Worse are the implausible third-hand tales of woe about someone's next-door neighbours' son-in-law's mother's friend who is now too scared to leave her own home after her unfortunate experience in Turkey where she was kidnapped at gunpoint, held for three days and fed only raw goats' meat. These ones are a bit like that fisherman's tale of the 'one that got away' – they get worse and worse each time they're told.

I have no idea why people think it's going to be at all helpful to tell you this stuff. It's not like you're going to learn a lot from it – some of it is pretty obvious, and you'd be able to avoid the same thing happening to you by applying just a little bit of common sense. After all, was the guy who left his clothes and cash on a Thai beach at 2 a.m. because he was drunk and thought it would be a good idea to go skinny dipping really all that surprised to find his stuff wasn't there when he got back? In most cases, unless you're unlucky enough to be in the wrong place at the wrong time (which you can't do anything about anyway), keeping your stuff and yourself safe is about not taking risks, being sensible, being careful and being alert. Do be on the look out, but don't be paranoid. Here's how.

KEEPING YOUR STUFF SAFE

To give yourself a good chance of making it round the world without having your bag, camera, passport, cash, etc.

stolen, you'll need to take care, be understated and do what you can not to make yourself an obvious target. If you look and behave like a tourist, especially a wealthy tourist, you're more likely to attract unwanted attention.

Secure storage

Having somewhere secure to store your things is a good start. In hostels, you may have access to a locker, so use it to keep safe things like your passport, tickets and possibly one of your cards which you won't need during the normal course of the day. You can also stash your iPod, phone, camera and other valuables in there overnight or if you're out and about and don't need them with you. In most places with lockers you'll have to supply your own padlock so make sure you've got a few spare locks with you. Combination locks are great because there's no danger of losing the key, but if your memory is terrible and there's a danger you'll forget the combination, you might be better off with a key lock. Just don't forget where you put the key. If the hostel doesn't have lockers, there is sometimes a safe available at reception that you'll be able to use. It's a bit of a pain to have to keep going back to ask for things, and you also have to remember that you can't access it when reception is closed, but as a minimum it provides safe storage for passports, tickets and spare cash.

Bank cards

If you can, take more than one card (credit and/or debit) with you and keep them separate. If you lose a card, or have one stolen, it's very easy to cancel it so that no one else can use it, but it's not so easy to get yourself a replacement card or access to any cash. If you've got a spare card kept separately, you can draw cash on that. And when I say keep two cards in separate places I mean totally separate, not just one card in your purse and one card in the bag you're carrying your purse in. If it's going to be stolen, it's just as likely to be the whole bag that gets taken, not only the purse. If your spare card is a credit card, remember that if you're drawing cash on it, it might attract additional interest charges. It's well worth having a chat with your bank before you leave home so you're clear about what conditions apply to your accounts, and what help will be available to you if you do have something lost or stolen while you're travelling. Also, if there's someone you trust at home, you could enquire about giving them third party access to your accounts so that if something goes wrong they can help you sort it out. It'll be a lot easier for them to do it for you in the UK, rather than you trying to make phone calls from Fiji or carry on email conversations from Ecuador.

Security when you're out and about

For safe keeping of your belongings while you're out and about, take a small shoulder bag or daypack with you for things you'll need to hand like your camera, purse, phone and sunglasses. Make sure this has a long strap so you can wear it diagonally across your body. If it's a backpack, in some locations – regrettably – you might actually need to wear it on your front. Yes, it probably will make you look like a geeky fourteen-year-old French exchange student, but in crowded streets or on public transport it's extremely easy for a thief to pickpocket a backpack. For extra security, invest in a small padlock to fasten the zip on your valuables bag. And never, ever, leave your bag on the floor next to your chair in a café or restaurant. Ideally make sure it's on your lap. Alternatively, thread the strap around the table or chair leg and then around your leg – although be aware that this doesn't stop someone cutting the strap and taking the bag anyway.

Just like it's a plan to keep your cards separate, it's also a good idea to have some cash hidden on your person as then if you do lose your purse or your bag, you'll still have some cash to get you back to wherever you're staying. Money belts or holsters can be useful for this, but having something so close to your skin can be uncomfortable in hot countries, or conspicuous under strappy tops. An alternative if you're wearing loose trousers or a long skirt can be to wear a money belt around your thigh, or even an elastic bandage with documents secured inside it. This also works well on overnight trains or buses if you're worried about the security of non-bulky items like your passport or cash. Stash a few folded notes inside your sock, or even better – and this is where for once we have an advantage over the guys – hide spare cash in your bra. Don't put coins in there though; it's really quite uncomfortable, not to mention startlingly cold when you first put them in.

STUPID THINGS I DID TO KEEP MY STUFF SAFE

I'll admit, I might have been a little on the paranoid side, but on the other hand I did manage to get all the way round the world without having anything stolen. I didn't wear any jewellery at all in South America, including a watch. I did wear my backpack on my front in some cities, especially when unloading off buses. And I was never more than about three inches away from my shoulder bag containing my camera, cash, cards and documents. That bag spent more time with me than I would have thought possible. I showered with it, I slept with it, I even shagged with it. That bag was practically welded to me – it felt like I'd have to have it surgically removed when I got home.

Despite my overcautiousness, I still had some moments of panic. For example, on arrival in Beijing, the driver of my taxi from the airport drove down a dark alley, stopped the car, got out and disappeared. Thinking I was about to be the victim of a taxi robbery, I sat there frantically trying to stuff my credit card down my knickers, thanking the gods that I wasn't wearing a thong. The driver got back in, started the engine and drove off – having just finished asking for directions.

While sightseeing in Rio de Janeiro, my pickpocket paranoia meant I spent an inordinate amount of time cannoning into strangers on overcrowded buses as I insisted on maintaining a vice-like grip on my shoulder bag with one hand and hanging on to the loose change in my pocket with the other hand. In most places this wouldn't be too much trouble, but in Brazil the bus drivers all think they're Ayrton Senna reincarnated. They take the racing line at corners without caring who they cut up in the process, they leave any required braking to the last possible second and screech to a halt at bus stops so as to arrive with smoking tyres, and they fling the bus round narrow bends for no reason other than to see how fast it's possible to take the bend without overturning the bus. As a result, Brazilian bus journeys were a very bruising experience.

How not to look like a tourist

Trying not to look like a tourist is another way to try to avoid being a potential victim of crime. For example, don't carry your camera around in a big camera-shaped bag emblazoned with Canon or Nikon or whatever other internationally known brand your camera is. If you do that, it'll be blatantly obvious that you're carrying an expensive camera and you'll be making yourself a target. And the problem with having your camera stolen is not that it's necessarily difficult to replace the camera (expensive yes, but challenging, not really – in most parts of the world, anyway), but that it is impossible to replace the memory card with your photos on it that's inside the camera. Also, especially in poorer countries, don't wear visible jewellery, particularly if it looks expensive. A street thief isn't going to stop to ask whether that watch is real gold or just gold plated.

Looking at maps in the street can also be like waving a big flag saying I'M A TOURIST on it. No one needs the deductive powers of Sherlock Holmes to figure out that if you're intently studying a map, you're probably new in town. To avoid this, plan your route before you leave your hostel and try to memorize it, or write a quick note of the directions on a small piece of paper for consultation in public. Remember the compass trick and try to ensure you're just heading in the right direction, even if you're not exactly sure which street to take. If you do need to consult your map, maybe pop into a café and sit down with it over a coffee or even just head into some public toilets where you'll be able to check it out without being quite so obvious.

Avoiding scams

To try to avoid being conned out of your cash, you need to be aware of the variety of scams that operate to fleece unwary tourists. Being forewarned is not necessarily a guarantee that it won't happen to you, but at least you'll have some idea what to look out for and alarm bells might start ringing, causing you to back off. This is a topic where the advice of family, friends and fellow travellers can be helpful. Your guidebooks will also be able to alert you to the more usual scams operating in the particular places you're visiting, so do give those a thorough read through before you hit the streets.

Scammers the world over are remarkably inventive. In China, for example, you may be approached by someone pretending to be a student who asks you to help them practise their English. They'll take you to a tea house and then after some conversation and a lot of different teas, they'll leave you with a rather large bill and a very angry proprietor. They'll then return later to split the profit with the tea shop owner. In Peru a pensioner may 'accidentally' spit on your shoulder and then pickpocket you at the same time as apologizing profusely and wiping it off. There are also stories of drugged food being offered for sharing on buses in Asia, bent police or customs officers in Asia and South America hiding drugs in your bag during a search, 'finding' them and then offering to let you off in exchange for a substantial bribe, and there are fake priests in India who charge exorbitantly for blessings and insinuate that unless you give them at least US$20 you clearly don't love your family all that much. To add insult to injury, after grabbing your cash, these priests decorate you with a flower garland and red pigment on your forehead so that all the shopkeepers then know you're a soft touch as well.

Sometimes, no matter how careful you are, your luck just runs out and something goes wrong. This happened to two of my friends while we were in Brazil. Totally a case of wrong place, wrong time – they got stuck in the middle of an art robbery and found themselves being forced at gunpoint to hand over their bags (containing all their cash, credit cards and passports). In that sort of situation, there's no point in trying to be a hero; your life is more important. Replacing all their stuff was a major hassle, but that's what travel insurance is for. Make absolutely sure you've got adequate cover.

Having said all of this, don't let the prospect of potential crime worry you too much and certainly don't have sleepless nights over it. Just be aware of the possible scams, try not to look like a tourist and keep your stuff as secure as you can. The likelihood of you being targeted when you're travelling is probably no higher than it is in London or any other big city; it's just that if it happens to you at home, it's a whole lot easier to sort it out because everyone speaks the same language as you and you're likely to have easy access to some funds, someone who can help you and alternative forms of ID.

DOs and DON'Ts of keeping your stuff safe

- DO pack lots of padlocks and use them to keep the critical stuff safely locked away.
- DO keep one card separate from the rest of your stuff, just in case.
- DON'T make yourself an easy target by carrying around shiny new logoed camera bags or wearing lots of bling.
- DO keep a tight hold on your stuff when you're in crowded places or restaurants.
- DO be careful who you take tea with in China.
- DON'T be fooled by fake priests and, if you are, DON'T wear the garland afterwards.
- DO make sure you've got good travel insurance.
- DO stash spare cash in your bra (or in your sock).

KEEPING YOURSELF SAFE

More important than looking after your stuff is looking after yourself. Objects you can replace, but you're unique.

Again, a dose of common sense is helpful. I'm going to sound like your mum for a bit again now and say that you probably wouldn't stagger half drunk around a city at home on your own at night, so don't do it when you're travelling. Make sure that if you're not in a group, you take a taxi and stick to well-lit streets where there are other people about. Don't be tempted to take shortcuts through dark, deserted alleys. OK, I've said it now, Mum mode off. If safety concerns you, check with your hostel before going out. They'll be able to tell you if there are any particular areas, streets or bars that are best avoided.

The importance of a map

First up, don't go anywhere without a map. I know what I said about looking at maps in public, but if you're lost, you have no idea where you are and you don't have a map, finding your way home could become a Krypton Factor-esque challenge. At the very least, you risk ending up with sore feet, having gone miles out of your way in the wrong direction; at worst you might end up in the wrong part of town and put yourself in danger.

I learnt about the map thing in Rio when a group of us went out sightseeing, got the wrong bus home and ended up somewhere unrecognizable. All we had between us by way of a map was a promotional leaflet for our hotel, with an imprecisely sketched picture of its immediate surroundings – designed to help you find the nearest corner shop and ATM, not to get you home from the other side of the city. What we should have done was get on another bus or get in a taxi. What we actually did was think we'd save some money and walk. We guessed a direction and set off, stumbling quickly into the middle of a *bloco* (an unofficial Carnevale street party). Initially, we thought it was quite fun, we thought we were experiencing the 'real' Rio: a seething mass of gyrating bodies, uncoordinated music blaring from stereos balanced precariously on window sills and rooftops, enterprising entrepreneurial teenagers with cool boxes full of drinks cans repeatedly calling '*Agua*, Skol*,*' men dressed in pink tutus, stray dogs and puddles of pee. We quickly realized that four white faces with blatantly no idea where they are or where they're going stand out like polar bears on a black sand beach. Dodging shouts of 'E, gringo' and 'I love you' and avoiding hands keen to fondle our virgin white skin, while keeping a close grip on bags and wallets, was not so much fun.

Part of the problem was that two of our group were blonde and six foot plus. It's pretty much guaranteed that if you've got blonde hair, in South America, Asia, the Middle East, the Mediterranean or Africa you're going to stand out. If you're also on the tall side, you'll be even more conspicuous – especially in Asia as the natives tend to be of small stature. Unfortunately, this may well mean that you attract a great deal of attention from men – not all of whom you may wish to encourage. If it bothers you, you could cover your hair with a hat or a scarf, or even dye it darker if you're staying a while and it's a serious annoyance.

SURVIVING A DAY IN DELHI

My arrival into Delhi at 2 a.m. wasn't promising. The guidebook said UNDER NO CIRCUMSTANCES should women take an airport taxi alone at night. It was quite definite about this point so I shelled out for a taxi arranged by the hotel. It didn't get any more promising as I was shown to my room – there appeared to be a tramp sleeping on a grimy blanket in a corner of the unlit hallway of the hotel. Nobody else seemed bothered, so once I'd ascertained that the room had a working lock, I decided I was too tired to care. After double-locking the door, barricading it with a complicated and very finely balanced arrangement of chair, bags and strategically placed coins (on the basis that if anyone tried to get in, the coins would fall to the tiled floor and make enough noise to wake me up), I went to sleep, hoping that it would all look much better in the morning.

The morning didn't get off to a good start with a cold shower in alarmingly brown water but, donning my most unattractive and tent-like piece of clothing and secreting money and valuables variously about my person, I nevertheless ventured out for breakfast, armed with my trusty guidebook and compass. Delhi is a scary city, especially if you're in the wrong part of it, which I most definitely was. No one bothers with niceties like pavements and road signs. What looked like ordinary roads on the map are tiny, dank alleys filled with rubbish, beggars and urinating men. One looks very much like another (the alleys that is, not the men), and without street names, there's no way to tell them apart. After twenty minutes of searching and no restaurant, I started to feel increasingly uneasy as I wandered through dusty heaps of rubbish and rubble, being stopped every two metres by extremely persistent Indian men asking me where I was going and how long I'd been in India, telling me it was very dangerous to go anywhere in Delhi on my own and offering to escort me in a taxi to their friend's restaurant/shop/hotel. Eventually, I was forced to abandon any attempt at politeness and, if they really weren't taking no for an answer, walk off while they were mid-sentence. (By the way, NEVER tell a man in the street that you've only just arrived in India; always say you've been there for three weeks.) I admitted defeat for the first time in eight months of travelling, went back to my hotel, locked the door, ordered room service and stayed there until it was time to join my tour group the next day. In Delhi, hunting in packs is definitely preferable.

Discouraging unwanted male attention

Trying to discourage male attention might not be your usual style, but if you are receiving unwanted advances from the locals, some of which could be quite crude, changing the way you're dressed might help. Take notice of what the local women are wearing. Clearly you don't have to wear the veil and a burkha, but if the women around you are mostly pretty well covered up, any flesh on display will attract attention. T-shirts might be better than vest tops, and trousers or long skirts rather than shorts. Be prepared – carry a light scarf or sarong with you that you can use to cover your shoulders or wrap around your legs. As well as making you feel a little more comfortable, covering up might actually be required when visiting certain temples or other places of interest. You don't want to miss out on a highlight by not dressing appropriately.

In these more modest locations, as well as covering up, choose loose clothing instead of tight-fitting outfits. In India, the more like a tent you look the better, as if you've got your assets on display in crowded public places such as markets, you could find yourself being treated exactly like a ripe melon – grabbed, fondled, caressed, groped and poked. In some of these countries, only prostitutes dress in revealing or tight-fitting clothing, so that's what you'll look like to the locals. Try to be aware of and respect cultural differences, and what messages you're sending by the way you're dressed.

To discourage men from bothering you in bars, as at home, a polite but firm 'No, thank you' should be your first tactic. If someone is more persistent and you're on your own, try to find a group of girls and ask if you can stay with them for a while in the hope he'll take the hint. Most women will be understanding and willing to help out in this situation, and if you find it difficult to shout this request over the music then you can always try talking to someone about it in the toilets instead. If a particularly persistent man just won't leave you alone, don't leave the bar. Instead ask the staff if they can call you a taxi.

Go with your instincts. If you're uneasy about someone, don't give them your number or tell them where you're staying, no matter how much they pester you. If you can't manage an outright no then be vague, make up a number, pretend you've forgotten your number and don't have your phone with you, take their number if you have to – just get them off your back. And definitely don't accept drinks from anyone you don't know in case they're spiked.

Travelling safely from the airport

Arriving into airports late at night is another possible risk area, as I found out in Delhi. Ideally, try to plan daylight landings for all of your flights. If that's not possible, check your guidebooks for advice on the safest method to get to your accommodation, and pay what it costs. Alternatively, stay in the airport until it's light, but that's a) not going to be much fun, and b) not going to be viable in an airport that's not open twenty-four hours. Your general anxiety levels will determine whether you choose to book accommodation in advance of your arrival but, to feel a bit more secure, it does help if you know where you're going when you get off the plane. When making your booking, ask the hostel's advice as to the best and safest way to get there. Some might even have their own transport, which could be free depending on how many nights you're staying.

Watch out for the typical airport pickup scam – your taxi driver tells you that your hotel is closed or double booked or just plain not a nice place to stay, and offers to take you somewhere else instead, or even to the 'Tourist Office' to make an alternative booking. He then takes you to his mate's hotel, who'll charge you five times the going rate and split it with your oh-so-helpful taxi driver. To avoid this, tell the driver that you're joining a tour you booked from

England before you left home and so you need to go to the hotel you were originally booked at in any case as you'll have to speak with the tour guide to find out what's happening. The magic words are 'booked in England' – that's the phrase that always seems to have the most impact and will usually stop even the most persistent drivers in their tracks. None of this needs to be true, of course; it just needs to work. In the unlikely event that you get to your hotel and find out that the driver was telling the truth and the place is a dump you can always get another taxi and go somewhere else, after consulting your guidebook for a recommendation.

DOs and DON'Ts of keeping yourself safe

- DON'T go anywhere without a map.
- DO cover up blonde hair if it's attracting attention that makes you uncomfortable.
- DO carry a sarong or light scarf to cover your shoulders or legs in case required.
- DO abandon normal rules of politeness if you feel scared or threatened.
- DO ask other women for help if you need to.
- DON'T ever admit to anyone that you only just arrived in India.
- DON'T hesitate to lie if it helps you avoid being conned or feeling threatened.
- DO book accommodation ahead if you're a bit nervous, or just like the security of knowing where you're going.

173

- DO remember that in most cases being polite but firm and insistent will get the message across and tell the person you're dealing with that you're serious about not being persuaded to do something you don't want to do.
- DON'T feel bad about hiding out in your room if it's all just too much.

MY SCARIEST EXPERIENCE

I've visited places notorious for violence, scams, muggings and pickpockets: La Paz, Rio de Janeiro, Cape Town, Johannesburg, Delhi, Nairobi . . . the list goes on. So, which of these was the scariest? Actually, none of them. The scariest thing that happened to me all year was an elephant encounter. Seriously. I was working on a game reserve in South Africa, doing game drives twice a day looking for lions, leopards, cheetahs and hyenas – all things which could do you serious damage. None of those bothered me. Instead, I collected a fear of elephants that will probably stay with me for life. Luckily, you don't find all that many of them in Winchester.

How come an elephant was scarier than anything civilization could throw at me? Quite simple. Any idea how fast an elephant can run? No? I had no idea either. In fact I didn't even know elephants could run until the day one took a strong dislike to the vehicle I was in, charged it twice and then full-on galloped down the road behind us as our rather nervous driver attempted a rapid getaway. It turns out that an elephant's top speed is about 45 kilometres per hour. That might not sound that fast, but wait until there's an elephant chasing you and you'll find out that it is pretty fast, actually.

As we raced through the reserve for nearly a kilo-
metre, pursued by a cloud of dust which occasionally
parted to reveal an extremely angry elephant, I sat curled
into a small ball on my seat, white-knuckled in my grip on
the bars of the truck. It was worse than any roller coaster
I've ever been on. Although I didn't want to look, I had
to. Glancing back nervously at the pursuing elephant, I
was screaming at the driver, banshee-like, to let him know
that now was not a good time to stop. I knew that if I lost
my grip I'd be flung out of the vehicle and trampled.
When it was finally over, I uncurled myself, shaking like
someone on speed doing the twist. My concern then was
for the safety of my fellow researchers. Their concern was
whether their video cameras had worked.

As if that wasn't enough abject terror for one day,
about three hours later I was walking with the rest of the
group up a koppie (small rocky hill) in the hope of boost-
ing our radio signal and helping us track the predators
we were supposed to be searching for. Instead, we
attracted the attentions of a huge bull elephant, slowly
and methodically making his way through the trees
towards us. The ranger instructed us to get to the top of
the koppie and hide behind the rocks. I sat there, hyper-
ventilating, my heart thumping like a jackhammer as I
watched a large elephant in full musth lumber very deliberately towards me. And as I'd learnt that morning, a
pissed-off elephant is not slow. (Musth, by the way, is a
hormonal episode causing an elephant's testosterone
level to rocket. During musth, elephants become excessively aggressive and territorial. Imagine the behaviour
of opposing football fans on a match day. An elephant in
musth is like that and with about as much rationality.)

I sat on top of that koppie, protected only by a ranger

with a rifle, contemplating death by elephant for the second time in a day. Should you ever find yourself in this position, the thing not to do is start to wonder whether it's even possible to stop an elephant with a rifle shot. That's a question that you only want to know the answer to if it's the right one. Those sorts of questions are best not asked at all. The answer, in case you're wondering, is that theoretically it's possible, but only if you hit exactly the right spot in a tiny target area on the elephant's head with exactly the right kind of bullet. If you miss, all you'll achieve is to wind the elephant up even more. Which is blatantly not a good idea. Luckily for us, the elephant decided that our side of the koppie was a little too steep for his liking so he lumbered off round the back of it to try to get at us that way, meaning that we were able to climb back down to our vehicle and make good our escape.

Still, it was the scariest thing that happened to me all year, so that's why, despite the 'high crime' cities I visited, the miles I travelled, the scams I avoided, and the survival skills required in Delhi, I still think an elephant is more terrifying than almost anything else you could throw at me.

Chapter Seven

PLANES, TRAINS AND AUTOMOBILES

Someone once said that the journey is more important than the destination. They were right. As a backpacker, you'll spend a considerable amount of time in various forms of transport, and sometimes it really is more about the experience than just about getting from A to B. It's often the journeys rather than the destinations that'll give you the stories you tell when you go back home. Travelling isn't just about arriving.

Getting about when you're on a budget involves a degree of creativity, and there's an element of taking almost anything offered to you as long as it's cheap. In the same way as you'll choose a hostel that's a bit of a walk from the action rather than pay a pound more to stay in the city centre, when it comes to transport, convenience is normally an inferior consideration. That's why, when I needed to go five hundred kilometres back to Perth and the bus journey would have taken three days, I instead accepted the offer of a lift in a road train (a really, really big truck). Getting into the cab was the hardest bit (they're SO high, it nearly required a block and tackle to get me in), but unless your man's a truckie, it's not something you're going to do every day. And by the way, great view from up there, do try it if you get the chance.

Some of the more standard forms of transport – like flights – are easy, but boring, so I'll give you some tips on keep yourself entertained through the tedium. Other means of travel are anything but boring, but as a consequence they're a bit more challenging. For those, I offer up some of my war stories in the hope that you'll fare better as a result of not repeating my mistakes.

IN THE AIR

In all likelihood, the furthest distances you'll cover will be in planes. A round-the-world air ticket is definitely the easiest way to see as much of the world as possible in what is a relatively short time, given the vastness of the planet. You can research routes yourself online but to purchase the ticket you'll have to phone an airline or pop into a travel agency. You can't purchase online because several airlines are involved. Sometimes it's easiest to get a travel agent to do the hard work for you in the planning stage when working out suitable routes and what type of ticket would suit you best. With round-the-world tickets there often isn't much difference between buying direct from the airline or buying through an agent.

Occasionally, you might be lucky enough to meet a traveller with other ideas – one who isn't doing the round-the-world ticket like everyone else. For example, I met a German guy who was doing his round-the-world trip entirely overland, so was completing all his major journeys

180

by sea. He was having a far more leisurely trip than most of the rest of us and was planning on travelling for three years. Believe me, you'd need three years to do a round-the-world trip by sea. If you meet such a traveller, do give them some airtime as they have some great stories to tell. Since I had neither the time nor the cash to be able to spend that long without working, I included twenty-three flights in my itinerary. As a result, I got very used to keeping myself amused during the waits involved in getting to the airport, waiting to board the plane, or flying for several hours.

Checking in

When it comes to getting to the airport, you've basically got two choices: get there early, or get there right at the last minute. If you get a bit nervous about these things and don't want to stress yourself out too much (like me), you'll probably aim to arrive the recommended three hours before take-off just in case there's a queue for check-in, or a queue for security, or a queue for passport control, or a queue for all three. You'll also probably significantly overestimate the amount of time it'll take to get to the airport in the first place – in case the bus is late, or there's a traffic jam, or the bus breaks down. Invariably none of these things happen so you actually arrive at the airport four hours before departure and then have to hang around, waiting for check-in to open and telling yourself with a forced smile that it's better to be early than late.

Once your city-to-airport journey has gone smoothly for ten flights in a row you might start wondering why you're always so cautious. You might even be tempted to join the last-minute brigade. Don't give in. On that one occasion when your bus does actually break down, your forward-panicking will be worth it. You'll still be stressed but you'll also be quietly proud that you've been so organized and have time to try and sort something else out.

If you don't fancy hours of hanging about and you have nerves of steel, the other option is of course to trust that everything will be on time, that everything will work fine and that there won't be any queues. If you're lucky enough to be one of these people, you can confidently believe that you'll arrive ten minutes before check-in closes, sail through security and passport control, get to the gate just before they put out a call for you and board five minutes before take-off. If you've got the constitution to do that, congratulations. If not, trying it is likely to result in an increased heart rate, a stressful and sweaty wait in the queue to have your bags X-rayed, an uncomfortably tense few minutes trying to figure out how to jump said queue without a) anyone noticing, or b) anyone assuming you're American, and then having to break the world 800-metre record as you sprint to the departure gate.

Keeping yourself amused while you wait

If you've gone for the safe option and arrived with time to spare, you're going to be waiting around. A lot. Yes, it is a bit boring but this is the one part of travelling where the destination is more important. Think about where you're going and it just might seem worth it. After a while, you'll be able to go into a sort of 'flight trance' and become a flying automaton, adept at ignoring the dragging passage of time as you queue to check in, queue to go through security, queue at the boarding gate, queue to get on the plane. Trust me, you'll be able to ignore the dull ache in your shoulders as you manfully wield your vastly overweight carry-on rucksack (full of all the things that were too heavy to put in your checked luggage), in what you hope is a nonchalant and carefree manner designed to ensure that no one actually puts it on any scales.

Tempting as it is to wander around window shopping, by doing so you'll risk spending money you don't have on tacky souvenirs. Instead, my advice is to get checked in, go through all the security procedures and get yourself to somewhere near the departure gate as quickly as possible. Grab a seat (as there are never enough and if you arrive late you'll either be sitting on the floor or standing) and then bury yourself in a very thick book, plug yourself into your iPod, or find a wi-fi hotspot and surf the time away. Read your guidebook for your destination if you like, and get excited about all the things you're going to be doing when you get there. Always visit the Ladies to avoid an uncomfortable start to the flight, remembering that there may not be any toilets at the gate itself. This is also the time to stock up on water. The rule about not taking liquids through security is a right pain, but there's nothing to stop you taking an empty bottle through and filling that up from a water fountain on the other side. It's cheaper than buying a replacement.

STRANDED IN MUMBAI
OR
WHY IT'S ESSENTIAL TO CONFIRM YOUR
FLIGHTS THREE DAYS IN ADVANCE

My flight out of India was much anticipated. I'd literally been counting down the days and then the hours until I could escape the dirt and the chaos. The evening before I was due to fly, I thought I'd just pop into an Internet café and check that all was in order with my flight. HORROR – the website showed no record of my flight. An expensive phone call to my travel agent back home elicited the information that my flight had been cancelled – three months earlier. Most helpfully, my travel agent had used the intervening time productively – by repeatedly emailing my self-evidently defunct former work email address to tell me about the change. I was booked on an alternative flight twenty-four hours later but that would mean I'd miss my non-amendable connecting flight out of Johannesburg.

Desperately seeking a solution, I phoned the airline, who advised me to check out of my hotel immediately, get a taxi through Mumbai rush hour to the airport and speak to one of their representatives who would try to get me on an alternative flight with one of their partner airlines. They told me this might mean I'd have to fly via Europe but as long as it didn't cost me any more and I got the connecting flight, I didn't care. I 'packed' in record time (by stuffing everything into fifteen carrier bags and deciding to worry about it once I had a flight to go on), checked out and sweated in a stuffy taxi in stop-start traffic. At the airport, I found the flaw in the plan. Which was, quite simply: no flight equals no representative at the airport. No one knew what to do with me. Trailing my luggage mountain behind me, I was sent to various unoccupied offices and desks on multiple floors of multiple terminals, directed by clueless security guards. Several more expensive international phone calls later, the airline eventually admitted that it had no idea why anyone would have told me to go to the airport in the first place and suggested that I abandon all hope of leaving India that night, go back to my hotel and sort it out in the morning. A fine plan, had my hotel not a) let my room out to someone else despite the fact that I'd paid for the night, and b) insisted they had no other vacancies.

So, as a result of a combination of my failure to confirm the flight well in advance and my travel agent's general ineptitude, I found myself stranded at Mumbai airport in the middle of the night. I seriously thought I'd be sleeping uncomfortably at the airport, with all my bags tied to my person and paranoid that something would get stolen. I was rescued by the kindness of strangers who offered the use of their mobile phones or spare change for the payphones. Desperate now, I phoned a girl I'd met in a café a couple of days earlier to see if I could crash on her floor for the night. She was a total star, squaring it all with the hostel and even staying up till I arrived to make sure they'd let me in. Even so, it wasn't a fun few hours. Don't be the person stuck in Mumbai – confirm your flights well in advance.

Keeping comfortable when flying

You'll want to be comfortable and keep yourself feeling fresh while you're waiting around at the airport and during the flight. Choose loose, comfortable clothes if you can, and go for layers so that if the air conditioning is Antarctic you can wrap up, but if it's Caribbean you can strip down a bit without giving the old duffer in the row opposite the thrill of his life. The added bonus of this is that the more items you're wearing, the less there is to pack – helpful if you've done too much souvenir shopping. The smarter you can manage to look, the better, as it means you'll attract less attention from officials. If you're kitted out in dirty, baggy trousers, a ripped T-shirt and a bandana, you might just find that you're the person who's 'randomly selected' for an extra security check – because the authorities will think you're a good bet to be smuggling something you shouldn't. Even though you're not, if you keep getting pulled for these checks it's quite annoying to have to repeatedly unpack and repack your bag, remove your belt and boots and then get dressed again and offer all your toiletries up for microscopic inspection.

Make sure you've got a comb handy along with some mints or chewing gum to keep your breath fresh, as well as a small bottle of moisturizer and some lip balm. The air conditioning on planes really dries your skin out. Remember to pack the moisturizer in a clear plastic bag to get through security without having it confiscated. Before and during the flight, drink plenty of water – you can always ask the cabin crew for extra water if you need to. With a wet wipe or two, much like on a long hike, you can strip down in the Ladies and give yourself a quick wash and freshen up. The little 'towelette' they give you with dinner will do if you forget to pack any wet wipes. After having your wash, apply some deodorant and the world will seem like a much better place. Admittedly, those toilets are quite small so washing in them can be challenging, but even if you can't face performing a Houdini-style contortion routine, just washing your face will make you feel so much better and less 'travel stained'.

In-flight entertainment

To kill time during the flight itself, your options are basically the entertainment provided (like movies or electronic games), a good book, sleep, or conversations with your fellow passengers. If sleep's your thing, the earplugs and eye mask you packed to help you get some rest in dorms will come in very useful. If you can't sleep, or want to try to avoid jet-lag and need to keep yourself awake, talking to people around you is a really good way to pass the time. You might get some interesting non-backpacker conversation and it's also your chance to quiz the natives for useful travel tips. Nobody has anything better to do on a plane so most people are happy to chat. And of course, after travelling for a while you'll be pretty good at striking up a conversation with someone you've never met before so that won't be a problem. It might be a chance to chat with someone you wouldn't have met otherwise. My mid-flight conversation partners included an exceedingly posh public-school-educated RAF officer, an Indian single mother living in Delhi and struggling to bring up her son and work full time without support from her family, and an Australian DJ heading out to Brazil to play on Copacabana beach during Rio Carnevale. You might pick up some helpful hints about what to see and do in the country you're headed for, or how to get the cheapest transport from the airport. You might even find someone who's staying somewhere near you to share transport with. You might find a drinking buddy for the next couple of days. All of which is far more useful than just finishing your Jodi Picoult. Although of course that is still an option if the movies are dull and everyone else is asleep.

If you're on a longer flight, you'll get fed. You might as well eat it since you've paid for it and it'll also help you avoid the nightmare of getting to your hostel at 3 a.m. starving but having to wait till it's light to go and find a shop or café. You may not think this now, but there could actually come a time when you start to look forward to airline meals; you know what you're going to get and your expectations aren't too high so you're rarely disappointed. Then there's the alcohol as well – a little bit might help you sleep, too much and you'll dehydrate yourself. Again, you've paid for it so you might as well indulge in moderation. If you like your in-flight drink, you might want to avoid flying with the national airlines of officially dry countries as they don't generally serve alcohol when departing those countries. The upside to this is that flights out of dry countries on other airlines do serve alcohol — and also tend to contain a substantial proportion of passengers who won't drink it. This combination means that if you are showing willing to drink it, the cabin crew seem to be keen to give it to you.

DOs and DON'Ts of comfortable, interesting and fresh-feeling flights

* DO confirm all flights at least three days in advance — especially on round-the-world tickets which have been booked months ahead.
* DO take a very thick book in case you've already seen the movies and there's no one awake to talk to.
* DO chat to your fellow passengers — it's not the London Underground; no one is going to section you for saying hello to someone you don't know.
* DON'T try to get through security looking like you're fresh from camping in knee-high mud at Glastonbury.
* DON'T book a flight out of a dry country on their national airline if you like your pre-dinner gin and tonic.
* DO remember to drink lots of water.
* DON'T forget to carry some wet wipes and breath mints so you can keep yourself feeling human.

OVER LAND

Flying is the quickest way to cover the most miles, but you'll see much more going overland. It's overland transport that'll give you the stories as well, whether it's improbable travelling companions or bizarre delays. Do look out of the window occasionally instead of just burying your head in a book, and if you're going to Australia, do try to get some time travelling through the outback. There really is nothing else like it. Overlanding will give you the chance to travel in ways you've never even heard of before. There are the standard overnight trains, jeeps, hikes, buses, cycle tours, ferry crossings, boat cruises and tram rides. Then there are the not so standard – converted Bedford trucks, rice barges, *songthaews*, auto rickshaws, cycle rickshaws, tuk-tuks, rickety Indian local buses, motorcycle taxis, helicopters, kayaks, light aircraft, lorries and, even more improbably, camels or elephants.

Some of these are so much more than just a means of getting about. They're part of the adventure, a must-do experience – even if it's one of those that you only 'must do' once. Take a *songthaew* for instance – quite frankly it could be the name of a tae kwon do move, but spend a while in Thailand and you will be riding around in them. In case you're wondering, it's an open-sided and open-ended pick-up truck with bench seats arrayed along the sides and complete with lights in the ceiling for travel after dark (fabulous for attracting the attention of a million biting insects) and an emergency stop buzzer (usually required as a result of someone having had too much to drink the night before). Travelling will offer you experiences like these – you never knew you were missing them, did you? Guidebooks and your fellow travellers will probably be the best sources to find out the cheapest or most efficient way to get to where you want to be, but remember: sometimes it's the journey, not the destination, that's important. You might want to occasionally take a train trip or ride something like a *songthaew* just for the experience. And why not – it's part of the fun.

PUBLIC TRANSPORT

I'll start with a word about buses. Buses are great. In principle. They take you from place to place and can get you a lot closer to certain localities than a train can, for example. But I just hate getting buses – not because you have to share a small space with people you don't know, or even because you sometimes get the nutter. Instead, it's my irrational fear of figuring out public transport systems in places I don't know. I can't even plead the language barrier, as I don't like it in England either. The problem I have with buses is that you need to know where you're going before you get there. If on the other hand you have no idea where you're going, you don't know when you need to get off. To be able to take a bus in a calm, dignified and relaxed manner, I have to have actually already been to where I want to get to at least once, because once I've done that, I know which stop I need.

My bus experiences typically involve me dragging back-pack, daypack and several additional carrier bags onto the bus, trying to find a seat large enough to balance me and all my worldly goods on it, then contending with mild panic attacks induced by the thought that either I've got on the wrong bus in the first place and am heading in totally the wrong direction or that even if I have managed to get on the right bus, I might miss my stop, go sailing past and end up several miles away from where I'm supposed to be with no possibility of a return journey until a week Tuesday. My bus anxiety wasn't improved by an Indian journey during which, after driving into a cul-de-sac and having to per-form a sixteen-point turn to get back out again, the driver was forced to admit that he had absolutely no idea where he was going and ask the passengers for directions.

If you're similarly nervous about bus travel, you can reduce your uncertainty by checking out a map before you go, sorting out where you're trying to get from and to and identifying any place names, areas or landmarks that you need to go through or past before getting to your destina-tion. Keep an eye out for these landmarks and reassure yourself that you're on track. You can also enlist the help of the driver and fellow passengers: plead absolute ignorance, flutter eyelashes and ask if they could possibly be so kind as to remind you when you get to XYZ place. In cities, you could also try to track your progress along the map in your guidebook, so at least if you end up in the wrong place, you'll know where you are, which is a good base for finding your way back to where you want to be. There are a few cities in the world where bus stops are labelled or colour coded, and some which provide specific public transport maps. If you've got to get on a bus, a quick visit to the tourist information office beforehand might save you a lot of sweating and stressing and wondering if you're on the right bus.

Trains

Trains and metro systems are (generally) a bit easier to use. They usually have the advantage of clearly signposted platforms and as long as you can read the map and the signs you're generally OK. And, unlike a bus, if you get on the wrong underground train, you can just get off a couple of stops down the line, cross the platform and go back the other way and start again. Except if you're on the New York subway, where not all trains stop at all stations on the line, so you need a bit of pre-planning and a decent map. The problem with trains tends to be not getting on the right one, but instead finding the right way to go once you're outside the station. That's where your compass comes in handy. Also, watch out for places where you have to stamp your ticket with the date before starting your journey. This sometimes happens on buses, trams or trains. If your ticket doesn't have a date printed on it when you buy it, you'll probably have to stamp it when you use it. If you don't, and you get caught, you'll be treated as if you don't have a ticket so you'll either have to get off, buy one and start again, or you might be fined and have to buy another ticket.

Overnight trains

Overnight trains are a different proposition altogether. It's an experience you really should have at least once in a lifetime if you want to call yourself a backpacker. They're often one of the cheaper ways to travel and they also save you the cost of a night's accommodation. Just don't make the mistake of thinking you're going to get a lot of sleep. Cattle-class backpacker budget overnight train trips in places like Thailand, China and India will offer not a lockable two-person cabin, but instead something more like a twenty-two-person cabin. A flimsy and ill-fitting curtain is likely to be all that divides your modesty from the well-used corridor. The luggage storage options will be either open racks, or shove-it-under-your-bed, which, incidentally, will be a plastic-coated fold-down seat that's approximately 70 centimetres wide. Imagine trying to sleep on a shelf and you'd be pretty close. The good news is, you can buy beer on board. The bar may well bear a strong resemblance to an empty carriage with a string of fairy lights across the ceiling and some bloke with a cassette player pretending to be a DJ, but if it sells beer, who's complaining? Drink enough of it and you won't even notice you're on a train (until you try to cope with the gentle swaying of the squat toilet).

Indian trains

Getting a train at any time in India, whether night or day, is (like so much of the country) both fascinating and frustrating in equal measure. Before you even make it onto the train, you have to get through lengthy delays, unexplained

194

platform changes and the frequent and unwanted attentions of beggars, gypsies and unaccompanied, wandering livestock. Indian Railways' ability to be late is unrivalled anywhere in the world. Stand on any given Indian train station platform for longer than ten minutes and you'll hear an announcement delivered in an unsurprised, deadpan tone that goes something like this:

'The 10.58 train to Mumbai is delayed by sixteen hours and seven minutes. Indian Railways apologize for any inconvenience.'

I love the fact that they tell you about the seven minutes. In the context of sixteen hours, seven minutes is supremely irrelevant.

Once you've made it onto the train, you'll find that they've sold far more tickets than there are seats. Abandon politeness – shove your way through the scrum and grab something to sit on. It's everyone for herself. Don't even think about stashing your luggage. There will be people sleeping in the luggage racks, so you'll be forced to try to curl yourself around your backpack, or abandon it to the floor. That's IF you can find any space amid the carpet of slumbering bodies. If you can, try to grab a top bunk (one of the few times it's a better option) as the bottom bunk is getting-groped territory. Try to persuade the boys to be chivalrous, and if that fails, bribe them with beer.

Keeping your luggage safe

If you're worried about the security of your luggage on overnight trains, you do have some options. You can buy a padlock with an extendable wire loop, and use that to lash your bag to something solid. You can use a bicycle lock if you have to. You can even invest in a 'pack-lock' if you want. It's a sort of wire net with a metal drawstring closure which envelops your entire backpack and then has a longer wire with which to lash it to a solid object. If you're really paranoid about your stuff, it might help you sleep easier. Opinion amongst my fellow travellers was divided about the benefits of this. Some thought that securing your bag so obviously would suggest to a would-be thief that there was something in it worth stealing and therefore would make it more of a target. I thought that instead of going to the bother of trying to cut through the wire, the would-be thief would simply take the unsecured backpack next to it instead. It's your call.

If you have something like this, using it does take a bit of planning. You need about fifteen minutes at the start of your journey to sort out your complicated arrangement of wires and padlocks, and then plenty of time to undo it again at the end before it's time to get off. I had one, and instead of sleeping soundly, secure in the knowledge that my luggage was safe, I'd spend the journey worrying about whether I'd wake up early enough in the morning to unlash it all and liberate my luggage before it was time to alight.

INDIAN RAILWAYS – NOTHING IF NOT POLITE

They may be unable to get their trains to run on time, but Indian Railways are at least polite. And they give you interesting signs to read during your lengthy wait. Like this one, found at Ajmer station:

**ATTENTION! DO NOT ENTER WITHOUT TICKET
BUY TICKETS AND TRAVEL WITH DIGNITY**

When you are in possession of proper tickets, you can travel with dignity and confidence. You enjoy your journey as your mind is at rest.

Without tickets, you are always afraid; you are unable to look at anyone with courage.

If you are caught, you are not only fined heavily but also become an object of ridicule and fun.

Why cheat yourself and the Nation, when you can travel honourably with a proper ticket?

Why indeed?

On-board entertainment

Keeping yourself entertained on overland public transport is generally much easier than on flights, if only as a result of the randomness of your travelling companions. Sometimes, the people you're sharing your space with are infinitely more fascinating than the view outside the window. Asia offers some of the most interesting varieties. Doing the rounds on Indian trains you'll find 'natural born eunuchs' selling their services and liberally cursing anyone who doesn't want them. (If you're wondering what a 'natural born eunuch' is, it's a boy who thinks he's a girl. The Indian collective psyche can't cope with the idea of transvestites so they've invented this interesting euphemism instead.) Well worth a look, but don't stare too hard or you might end up the subject of one of the curses. India is also your place if you've ever wondered what it would be like to share a bus journey with a goat. If, on the other hand, you've ever fancied either getting a taste of the celebrity lifestyle or imitating a goldfish, take a train in China. You'll be the main attraction, with everyone staring at you, wanting to know why you're there, how long you're staying and what you think of the country.

Sightseeing on foot

Alternatively, you could just walk, if grappling with timetables, uncertain destinations, overcrowded trains or the nutter on the bus isn't your thing. You might even manage to talk yourself into believing that you actually prefer to stroll around the city than drive around it. After all, you get the chance to take in the atmosphere, see a little street life, appreciate the unique local sights and smells, check out the interesting architecture or soak up a bit of the culture. Exploring on foot is a great idea, although it has its risks. It's never quite as panic-inducing as the bus journey into the unknown but it can still be surprisingly hazardous at times.

In some countries, merely crossing the road requires all the fear and daring of a bungee jump. It's just much cheaper. Take China, for instance – pedestrians are the lowest of the low. In the pecking order, if you're on foot, you're at the bottom. Any other traffic can do exactly what it wants. Bicycles and scooters in particular seem to be exempt from any and all traffic regulations. They can ride on whichever side of the road they like or even take to the pavement if the road's a bit congested. Be prepared for cyclists or scooter riders to honk aggressively at you for inconsiderately walking in their pathway, especially if you're on the pavement. They'll also ignore red lights all together. In China, the presence of the green man is not an indication that it's safe to cross, it's merely a suggestion that there may be marginally less traffic hurling itself at you than will otherwise be the case. Remember all those road safety videos you had to watch when you were little? Apply your Green Cross Code. Stop, look and listen – then charge across the road like Usain Bolt finishing the 100 metres, weaving between the traffic as you go. If you make it across without any honks, give yourself a point.

Local transport

When your feet are tired and sore, or it's just too far to go, try something a little different like a tuk-tuk, a cycle rickshaw or even a motorcycle taxi (go on, I dare you). If you venture to India, be warned that the traffic there is as mad as its Chinese counterpart. Your first ride in an auto rickshaw will terrify you, but trust me, you get used to it very quickly since there's not a whole lot of choice. After just a few days you'll be able to sit in an auto rickshaw without swearing, ducking and pressing your foot to a non-existent brake pedal every three seconds. You'll sit serenely, calmly and disinterestedly watching as your driver narrowly misses colliding with another vehicle, then swerves violently to avoid a cow standing in the middle of the road while driving the wrong way round a roundabout. You'll be unsurprised that during all of this he'll keep up a stream of persistent enquiry as to whether you can visit his brother's shop on the way home.

It's a truth universally acknowledged that every auto rickshaw or cycle rickshaw driver in India has a brother who owns the best/cheapest/most honest shop in town, and that that shop is always conveniently located 'on the way home' no matter where you're coming from or going to. The driver will be at pains to reassure you that 'looking is free' and that you're only going there 'just for looking'. The resultant negotiations as to whether you are or are not going to visit the aforementioned shop will always be of far more concern to your driver than keeping his eyes on the road, so close them down with a firm 'NO'. Once won't be enough; you'll need to be persistent. Don't waver for a minute, or he'll take advantage of your weakness. If necessary, tell him that you're going straight back to your hotel, not to a shop, and that if he's not prepared to do that could he please stop the rickshaw now and you'll get out and find someone who will. Usually, they won't want to lose the fare, so will give in to what you want, but if not, follow your threat through, get out, walk around the corner, then hail another driver and try again. There are more auto rickshaws in Delhi than Imelda Marcos had shoes, so trust me, getting another one won't be a problem.

THE TERRIFYING ORDEAL OF THE MOTORCYCLE TAXI

Perhaps ill-advisedly, I chose Brazil (not a nation known for its health and safety standards) for what was my first ever experience of two wheels. It was a budget-dictated choice – the cheapest available option to get me from the campsite to the town, five kilometres away. It started badly as the driver presented me with a strapless crash helmet and, without waiting for me to get a decent grip, roared off down the unmade red dirt road. Wearing no protective clothing whatsoever (apart from the completely useless helmet), I found myself idly wondering whether I'd be covered under my travel insurance if an accident was to occur. (I never did find out the answer to that one – you might want to check it out if you think you'll be in the same position.) As if that wasn't enough, with immaculate timing, my subconscious mind dredged up a remarkably clear re-run of a motorcycle safety video shown to me at school. That had demonstrated in full Technicolor glory the serious and disfiguring injuries it is possible to inflict upon oneself when travelling on a motorbike without proper protective clothing.

Consequently, it was not a comfortable ride. It got a lot worse when we were about halfway to town and my driver decided to start some sort of race with his mate. This seemed to involve weaving around each other, achieving the closest possible proximity without actually touching – a version of chicken in which you're both travelling in the same direction. To complete my misery, just before we arrived to town the heavens opened, soaking me to the skin and turning the road instantly to mud.

> Since there were no mudguards, I ended up with a delightful orange muddy stripe right up the middle of my back. I looked like a petrified badger advertising easyJet.
>
> The purse took a hit on the way home – I paid the extra for a proper taxi.

DRIVING YOURSELF

If you don't fancy being under someone else's direction, you can always find your own transport. Sometimes you can get a good deal on a hire car and it can work out quite cheap if there's a group of you. Also, keep an eye on car hire companies' websites as sometimes if they need a car relocated you can get it for free and just pay the petrol, providing you take it from where it is to where they want it to be within their timescale. Alternatively, lots of backpackers in Australia and New Zealand actually buy a car if they're there for more than a couple of months as it works out cheaper than hiring one, since you can sell it on and get some of your money back once you're done. Of course, you risk buying a basket case that breaks down every five minutes, but make the relatively cheap investment of joining a breakdown service and help will be at hand even if the worst does happen. Unless you're somewhere without mobile phone reception of course . . .

The toughest thing about driving unfamiliar cars is that they're, well, unfamiliar. When I had to hire a car in New

202

Zealand, where almost every car is automatic, I was a bit concerned about the fact that I'd never driven an automatic before. So, what do you do when you need to know something about a car? That's right, you ask your dad. Even if he is on the other side of the world. As usual, he gave me some fantastic advice, so just in case you need them too, here are my dad's instructions on how to drive an automatic:

Automatic drive – not a problem. All you have to remember is to keep your left foot on the floor and completely away from the pedals. If you can pin your left foot to the floor, do so!

There is no clutch so you don't need a left foot – remember this all the time.

What do you have to remember?

Keep your left foot on the floor and do not put it on or anywhere near the pedals – remember this and driving an automatic is easy.

Remember, do not use your left foot – OK?

If you don't remember this you will find yourself braking very, very sharply as you try to declutch on the foot brake. To declutch in a normal drive car, mostly it is normal to push the clutch pedal close to the floor. If you use your left foot in an automatic you will place it on the brake pedal and, as I say, the car will come to a very abrupt halt – possibly in front of the car behind, who – rather surprisingly – will not be expecting you to stop so suddenly and therefore there is the risk of what us hetero-

sexual males fear the most: a 'tail-end shunt'!

So remember, KEEP YOUR LEFT FOOT ON THE FLOOR AND AWAY FROM THE PEDALS.

Right – now that is firmly in your head, the next thing is to use the handbrake when you want to pull away on an incline. Handbrake on; right foot on the 'gas' pedal. Where is your left foot? That's right, you remembered – it is on the floor! Gently increase the revs on the gas pedal and let off the handbrake; increase the gas as you pull away. It is a bit like riding the clutch on a normal drive car, except you will not be using your left foot as there is no clutch pedal and your left foot is firmly fixed to the floor – OK?

I remembered this excellent advice and had no problems at all with my left foot. I did, however, have quite a lot of problems with the fact that the indicators were on the opposite side, resulting in me furiously wiping my windscreen every time I took a corner.

DOs and DON'Ts of overland transportation

- DON'T beat yourself up about travelling on buses if it scares you. Instead, give yourself enough time and the right shoes to be able to see cities on foot, and congratulate yourself on the amount of architecture and culture you've seen.
- DO remember to buy a ticket – take Indian Railways' advice and travel with dignity.
- DON'T expect that just because you're on the pave-

ment in China you're safe. Remember that pedestrians are fair game, have no right to be anywhere near the road and that bicycles and scooters clearly take priority – even on the pavement.

- DO leave European notions about road safety at home. You'll only scare yourself if you take them with you.
- DON'T use your left foot when driving an automatic.
- DO be firm with persistent Indian auto rickshaw drivers.
- DO ask your dad's advice if there's anything motoring or mechanical that you're just not sure about.

Chapter Eight

INTERNATIONAL RELATIONS

One of the great things about travelling is the new people you meet. Or so you'll be told. And you WILL meet some really fantastic and really interesting people, some of whom will become friends for life. Sadly, though, the law of averages means that you'll also meet some really irritating or really bizarre people as well. Laugh at them, but don't worry about them – one of you will be moving on in a few days. As you travel you'll meet, chat and share space with other travellers, officials and, of course, the natives. You'll have to overcome language barriers and cultural differences, and you will – with varying degrees of success and amusement on the way. The thing to remember is to go for it – it's entirely likely that you'll never have to see these people again so if you make an absolute arse of yourself it doesn't matter. Just keep smiling and chalk it up to experience. In this chapter I'll give you the recipe for the basic backpacker conversation, give you some hints to help you avoid cultural cock-ups and talk about the obvious and not so obvious language barriers and how to get round them.

FELLOW TRAVELLERS

Obviously, the people you'll be spending the most part of your time with are your fellow travellers. Staying in hostels will automatically provide you with a rapidly changing cast of characters to mix with. You might not think so now, but in hostels it's very easy to meet and chat to strangers; whether in your dorm, in the kitchen or in the bar, most people will be happy to engage in conversation if you approach them with a friendly smile. If you're travelling on your own don't be worried about being lonely, because you won't be. A person on their own is much more approachable than a group or a couple, so you'll probably find that people will start talking to you without you having to make too much effort. If not, just smile and say a friendly hello when you walk into your dorm, or the kitchen – see who smiles back, go over and introduce yourself and, hey presto! – conversation. Even if you're a bit shy, don't worry; after spending a bit of time travelling you won't be shy anymore. Plus, you kind of have to make the effort because if you don't, you'll spend days on end talking to no one but bus drivers, which can get a touch tedious.

How to talk to strangers

Worried about what to say? There's no need to be. Basically, what you actually say is less important than the fact of starting up a conversation. Have some general

210

'approach phrases' to use so you don't have to give it too much thought. Something like, 'Hi, how are you?' or 'Hi, my name is. . .'. It's not speed dating; you don't get points for originality. If you happen to be in the kitchen, making a comment about what someone's cooking can be an opener. If that person is interested in chatting, you'll find that the conversation moves on from there. You might even end up sitting down to eat together, maybe sharing a bottle of wine.

You'll realize after a while that there's a Standard Backpacker Conversation you'll find yourself repeating (with minor variations upon the general theme) all over the world. You'll lose count of how many times you'll have this conversation – and yes, it does get a bit repetitive after a while – but the good thing about the Standard Backpacker Conversation is that you don't have to think too hard about it, it helps you meet people and it gets you chatting.

Basic recipe for the Standard Backpacker Conversation

INGREDIENTS
Names
Countries of origin
Where you've been
Where you're going
How long you've been travelling
What you thought of ABC place, XYZ place

METHOD

Step 1: Greet (e.g. say 'Hi') and give your name.

Step 2: The other person replies with their name.*

Step 3: Ask where they're from.

Step 4: They reply, then will usually ask you where you're from.

Step 5: Tell them where you're from, then ask how long they've been travelling for.

Step 6: They reply, then repeat the question back to you.

Step 7: You answer, then ask where they've been so far.

Step 8: They give you a rundown of the places they've visited and turn the question back to you.

Step 9: You reply. If they've been somewhere you've been or somewhere you're going, pick it out and ask them what they thought of it . . . (conversation continues).

* If you fail to elicit a response at Step 2, they either don't speak English or don't want to chat. Give it up right there, return to Step 1 and try again with someone else.

So you can see what the finished article looks like, here's one I made earlier:

'Hi, I'm Chelsea.'

'I'm Anna.'

'Where are you from, Anna?'

'Sweden, how about you?'

'England. How long have you been travelling for?'

'Four months so far. You?'

'Six months. I'm travelling for a year all together.'

'Where have you been so far?'

'South America, New Zealand, and now I'm here. How about you?'

'Thailand, Fiji and New Zealand. I'm going home via America.'

'What did you think of Thailand? I'm going there next.'

(And so on…)

You see? I promise, it is actually really easy. And, because you don't have to think too hard about what you're going to say next, you can concentrate on listening to what the other person has to say and finding some common ground or identifying something to talk more about. Remember, this is only the basic recipe. You can add in new ingredients, or wander off on a slightly different tack if the conversation takes you that way. For example, if one of you has visited the other's home country, you might make a few complimentary comments about it, or if your conversation partner is a fellow country(wo)man you'll probably find out that one of you has relatives living somewhere near the other's home town, that there is some other tenuous possibility of shared acquaintances or another improbable connection.

As I said, these conversations do get a bit repetitive after a while, but it's worth persevering. Sometimes they elicit useful information and recommendations for somewhere that's in your future itinerary, sometimes they find you someone to have a drink or hang out with for a couple of days. You might find that you're headed in the same direction and you can maybe share transport to your next destination, or you might meet someone you get on well with, stay in touch and meet up with again later on. The possibilities are, as they say, endless.

How to spot different nationalities

Being able to identify different nationalities without having to ask is a useful skill to acquire – it helps keep you amused when there's not a lot else to do and it can also help you to avoid offending someone by guessing their nationality wrong. Kiwis are quite used to being mistaken for Aussies but they'll be pleasantly surprised if you do manage to get it right. Canadians and Americans, on the other hand, are unlikely to be so understanding. And quite frankly, you can understand why a Canadian would be upset about that one. To help you avoid tripping up, here's what to listen out for:

South Africans: spot these by a harsh-sounding nasal twang and a tendency to promise to do things 'just now' then not get on with them. In South Africa, 'just now' means 'at some point in the next three months'. (If you want them to do it straight away you have to specify 'now now'.) Also worth remembering that Zimbabweans sound remarkably similar to South Africans but generally don't mind if you get it mixed up – at least you've got the right continent.

Australians: listen out for sentences going up in tone at the end, so that they sound like a question even when they're not. Can also be identified by liberal use of the greeting 'G'day', by referring to everyone as 'mate' or by offering other people 'tinnies'.

Kiwis: like Aussies, everything they say sounds like a

question, but to tell them apart, check out the vowel sounds. Kiwis (unlike Aussies) tend to switch their vowels around when they talk. For example, the letter 'a' sounds like an 'e' when pronounced by a Kiwi, so the English word pack is pronounced 'peck'. Similarly, 'e' becomes 'i' so eggs are 'iggs'. And 'i' becomes 'u' so pin becomes 'pun'. This vowel swapping results in the infamous 'fush end chups'. Kiwis are also conspicuous for overuse of the words 'awesome' and 'sweet', suffixing adjectives with 'as' for no apparent reason (as in 'sweet as', 'tough as') and they also have a tendency to finish sentences with 'eh'.

Americans: listen for the boastful swagger of that accent, which should be enough of a giveaway. If not, Americans can also be identified by a tendency to be very loud and to dominate whatever conversation they're in. Also distinguished by the peculiar phrase 'good job' which appears to be a form of praise (although to me it sounds precariously close to discussing matters best left in the restroom), and if they're from the South, use of the word y'all (a contraction of 'you all') to address either individuals or groups. As in, 'How y'all doing?'

Canadians: to the rest of the world, Canadians sound like Americans. They appear to be quite distressed about this. In an effort to differentiate themselves, they often sew a Canadian flag onto their backpack, so that's something to look out for. Also, if they sound like an American but combine this with the Kiwi habit of ending their sentences with 'eh', they're definitely Canadian. If you are in any doubt regarding American or Canadian, it's usually safer to opt

215

for Canadian as Americans (at least those who travel abroad) tend to be less offended at being mistaken for a Canadian than vice versa.

A WORD ABOUT CUSTOMS

And I don't mean the local folk dance or welcome drink. Your guidebooks will help you negotiate your way around those without too much trouble. Instead, I'm talking about the customs officials who'll be the first people you meet when you arrive somewhere new. Ambassadors for their country they usually are not – although in developing countries they may be very interested to have a chat with you about where you've been, what sort of work you do at home and so on. Humour them, they usually just want a chat as their days are quite dull – they'll stamp your passport and wave you on without any problems. American customs on the other hand are a different beast altogether. They're so paranoid it's scary. They'll make you feel like a criminal even though you know you're innocent. Be polite, be patient, answer questions sensibly and clearly and, above all, try not to be smart. Yes, even if they're winding you up. Grit your teeth and keep smiling. It doesn't pay to get aggressive because if they decide they don't like you, they can make your life very difficult indeed.

Unless you've done something really silly, the only other customs you're likely to get entangled with are Antipodean, since they're anal beyond belief. Both Australia and New

Zealand are *über*-protective of their agriculture and eco-systems and, as a result, food, soil and plant material receive the same level of scrutiny as you would normally expect for class A drugs. Try not to laugh – they take this stuff very seriously indeed.

Here's how to secure safe passage through customs with minimum disruption:

- Fill in arrival forms and customs declarations clearly, in pen. Don't cross anything out. If you make a mistake, get a new card and start again.
- Don't try to hurry the officials, even when they are being irritatingly slow and you've got a transfer flight to catch. If you look like you're in a hurry, they'll deliberately take twice as long.
- Declare EVERYTHING – if you're unsure about whether you need to declare it or not, it's better to declare it and have them decide that you didn't need to than not declare it and get hauled up for it. For example, in Australia and New Zealand you have to declare any food you have with you. As I found out the wrong way, this means anything at all that is edible – a packet of sweets, a chocolate bar, your pot of Marmite . . . The first time I went to Australia I failed to declare a bag of jelly sweets and got hauled off for a sweaty few minutes of wondering whether they were going to put me on the next plane back home. They didn't, but it showed me that the consequences of not declaring something that you should have declared can be time-

consuming and embarrassing. If they find something you didn't declare, they'll go through everything in your bags and examine it in minute detail. Believe me, you really don't want to have to explain to a customs officer with a sense of humour bypass exactly what your vibrator is and what it's used for.

- Check customs regulations well before you arrive – in fact, before you even pack, to make your passage easy. If there's anything they need to inspect, pack it at the top of your rucksack so it's easily accessible. In Australia and New Zealand, this means anything that might have soil on it such as tents or hiking boots, as well as food.

THE NATIVES

Opportunities to meet the natives can be brilliant. You'll get to know and understand the lifestyle and culture of a place much better with the locals than with a bunch of other travellers. Sometimes you might have an opportunity to do a home stay, go on a tour or trek to see more remote native communities, or more prosaically, you'll just interact with people on the streets, in shops and bars and restaurants. Alternatively, if you're staying somewhere for a while and have the right visa you might be able to live and work in a different country, which offers a very different perspective to simply travelling around it.

Culture shock

One of the reasons why travelling is so much fun is that not everyone handles things the way we do. As I've already shared with you, Delhi requires a certain amount of tolerance along with the ability to dodge livestock and walk past piles of poo as if you do that every day and it's nothing out of the ordinary. The streets of India are at least very obviously different from home, so that gives you a bit of a clue to expect a certain degree of unusualness. Less obvious, but potentially more challenging, are countries which look civilized and fairly similar to home, but actually are very different; China being a case in point. China has a liberal sprinkling of Western chains such as McDonald's and Starbucks, ritzy shopping malls and a profusion of neon lights, but underneath all of that, Chinese cities can still be bewilderingly unfamiliar, and not just because all the writing looks like little pictures.

Interactions in Chinese public places are vastly different to most of the rest of the world. When you first arrive, you feel like you've walked into the most impolite society on earth. People shove past you on the streets, aggressively pushing you out of the way. In the subway, you'll be elbowed and jostled and people will push in front of you in queues with no apparent concern. Getting on or off a train is particularly challenging. There's no concept of queuing or waiting in turn. People on the platforms simply stuff themselves into the train as soon as it opens its doors. You'll be dragged forwards and backwards in a heaving tide of bodies, battling the conflicting forces of those trying to barge their way onto the train and those desperately trying to leave it. You'll also find that people will stare at you, openly and wherever you go, which can be quite disturbing. When I visited the Terracotta Army a group of Chinese businessmen were more interested in having photos taken with me and my room-mate than they were in looking at the amazing statues, and after spending ten minutes sat in a minibus outside a Chinese railway station during which we drew a small crowd of staring locals, I have a degree of empathy with goldfish.

This will be slightly less bewildering if I explain that Confucian theory, which has had a huge influence on the Chinese culture, teaches that rules of politeness and courtesy are only applicable to family, friends and acquaintances. This means that it is therefore perfectly socially acceptable and not in the least bit impolite to push, shove and elbow strangers if they happen to be in your way. The same rules also mean that queuing is unnecessary – it's every man for himself. Once you've figured this out, you're liberated. You can join in with the pushing and shoving with absolute impunity since everyone in the country is a stranger to you, so you don't need to be polite to anyone. Throw yourself into the general mêlée with gusto and enjoy the experience, especially if you're taller than the average Chinese. Your superior height will give you an advantage in the shoving and elbowing stakes. Watch a sea of Chinese part before you, and get an idea what Moses must have felt as he divided the Red Sea.

Working abroad

Living and working in a country gives you a very different picture from the one you get when you're just passing through on a visit. Doing a bit of work as you travel is not only about propping up your bank balance and funding onward travel, it's also a great way to take some time out and stay in one place for a while, meet the natives and learn a bit more about the country you're in. The easiest bets for work are bar or farm work, waitressing or fruit picking, but if you're in a city you might be able to get office work if you've got experience. Farm work or fruit picking can usually just be picked up locally by reading notice boards at supermarkets or hostels. Alternatively, if you're looking for bar or office work, prepare your CV before you go and have lots of copies to hand out. Pound the streets and hand it in to anywhere you're interested in working, and register with lots of agencies as well to cover all the bases.

ON THE PULL IN HICKSVILLE, WESTERN AUSTRALIA

During my second visit to Australia I decided I wanted to experience life out in a small town in the middle of nowhere – the kind of place where if you ran out of milk then that really was that until next week's delivery. To which end, I went 'on the pull' by getting a bar job in the People's Republic of Western Australia, the state that's so far away from anywhere else that it's like a country in its own right. I had a romantic dream of ending up in a nice colonial pub, all lace ironwork and weatherboards with an ever-changing clientele of international travellers eagerly exploring the highways and byways of outback Australia and passing their evenings sharing interesting stories around the fire. Instead, I found myself at the Jerramungup Motor Hotel, an uncompromisingly ugly 1960s establishment decorated with fantastically clashing lino and playing host to farmers, shearers and labourers. Luckily, the only thing I was interested in pulling was the pints.

Jerramungup (or Jerry, to the locals) is 500 kilometres east of Perth. It's a town so small that it doesn't have an ATM and the local library prints its own postcards of the local sights. Highlights: the school and a sheep. And that is about as exciting as it gets. A big Saturday night out in Jerry is frozen pizza and darts in someone's garage while singing karaoke into a child's toy guitar. My arrival caused some degree of excitement in the town. On the loose was a single, unattached female who wasn't related to anyone already living there. If you're looking to pull a bit more than pints, this kind of town is the place to be – especially if you like a bit of rough. For really good odds to score, get a job in a mining town where guys normally outnumber girls about twenty to one.

Working in the pub was an experience I'll probably never forget. It was a pub, restaurant, off-licence and betting shop and pretty much the only place in town to get alcohol. Opening hours depended on the number of patrons, so sometimes on a Monday we'd be closed by 7 p.m. On a Saturday we could still be going strong at 4 a.m., though. Despite never having worked a bar before, they took me because I could speak English. As a result, I'm probably the only barmaid in the world who can't pull a pint. The Jerry Hotel doesn't serve pints as the landlord insists that the fridges aren't big enough to store pint glasses. (Yes, that's how anal the Aussies are about cold beer – even the glasses are kept refrigerated.)

I must admit, it took me a while to get the hang of pulling a beer the Aussie way. I'm used to the English way: making sure the beer comes all the way to the top of the glass so you can't be accused of giving short measures. Aussies, on the other hand, aren't happy unless they've got a head the size of a small iceberg on their beer. The bar etiquette also took a bit of getting used to. It was remarkably complex. I was expected to know all the locals' names and what they drank so as to be able to greet them and have their beer waiting for them on the bar as soon as they walked in the door. When a punter finished his drink he'd place the empty glass back on the bar. If he stood the glass up, he wanted another drink – I had to remember what he was drinking and refill it. If he laid the glass down, though, that meant he'd had enough for the night. The men would also leave little piles of change dotted around on top of the bar so I had to remember whose money was whose, take it from the correct pile and replace the change. Thus, the entire transaction often took place without the drinker experiencing the inconvenience of having to break off from his conversation at all. Business was highly erratic – our busiest times were when it rained, as apparently you can't shear wet sheep.

It's funny what you learn when you're travelling.

Dating

Whether you're interested in dating or just shagging will probably depend on how long you're in town and how many points your mates will award for each different nationality you get through. If you're after a quick one-nighter, backpacker bars are *the* place to hang out (especially if you're looking to increase your nationality count). They'll either be full of backpackers, who are mostly looking for the same thing as you are, or they'll be full of locals who've figured out that that's what to go there for. Either way, you're on to a winner. Aussie men are particularly easy to pull. Hang around for a while and if he offers to buy you a beer, he's actually saying he wants to take you to bed. If you accept the beer, you're also agreeing to sleep with him later. If the horizontal tango is your aim and you're sharking in a bar, try not to drink too much yourself as when you head off with your pull you don't want to be so drunk you don't know what you're doing, nor do you want to throw up on him. *Not* a good look.

Alternatively, check out Gumtree on the Net – there are always plenty of people on there looking for a good time. Gumtree, for the uninitiated, is a website used a lot by Aussies and Kiwis, especially those in exile. It's a kind of giant Web-based noticeboard filled with Wanted or Offered ads, including personals. Some of the offers it makes you'll probably want to avoid (or at least I know I'd steer clear of the ones from married men 'in the city for one night only and looking for someone to keep my bed warm') but there are some less sleazy ones on there. If you choose to meet up with someone you've made contact with on the Internet, make sure that it's in a public place and that someone knows where you are and when you're coming home.

If you're more in for the long haul and are going to be in town for a while then something a little more sedate might be on. If dating's your aim, meet people in bars or through friends; try speed dating or Internet dating; or join a singles club or sports club. Just remember when you meet up with someone for the first time that you're far away from home and there's probably no one looking out for you. Tell someone who you're meeting and where you're meeting them, even if you have to text that information to your mate back at home. And when you get back after your date, let that person know you're back safely to avoid them activating a search party.

Whether you're in it for a quick fix or some longer-term fun, you know what I'm going to say next, don't you? Yes, that's right. DON'T FORGET THE CONDOMS. Although of course you listened to my advice in the Health chapter regarding their availability (or otherwise) so you've already got some in your bag and some in your bra. Haven't you?

DOs and DON'Ts for dealing with people

- DON'T get bored with the Standard Backpacker Conversation. It's an easy way in, and this time you could be talking to your next drinking buddy or someone who knows something useful about the place you're heading to next.

- DO remember my handy guide to Kiwi vowel pronunciation – it helps to avoid confusion when someone directs you to the chicken disk at the airport.
- DO declare absolutely everything that might remotely fit into one of the categories on the customs card. Chocolate does apparently count as food.
- DON'T be tempted to laugh or be smart with irritatingly officious customs officers as they'll just waste even more of your time.
- DO find out about and follow the local customs. For example, when in China, do as the Chinese do. Push, shove and jump queues like a rebel – and enjoy it.
- DO remember than Aussie men like head – and that their beer had better be cold.
- DON'T forget the condoms.

LANGUAGE BARRIERS AND OTHER OPPORTUNITIES FOR CONFUSION

With the little bit of French, German or Spanish you learnt at school, you should be able to get around Europe without too much difficulty. Nearly everyone speaks English anyway. Language-wise, English-speaking former colonies are also easy – yes, even India. In Thailand you'll be surprised by the amount of English spoken and you'll find that road signs and menus are generally available in English. The problem comes when you're off the beaten track a bit, in places like Russia, China and South America where almost no English is spoken. It's even harder if they use a different alphabet so you can't read the signs. A phrase book might help you out, but failing that you might need to get a local guide.

As a minimum, wherever you are in the world it's a good idea to try to learn how to say 'thank you' in the local language (to be polite), and to try to remember the respective words for 'Ladies' and 'Gentlemen' just in case there aren't any pictures (to save your blushes). If English words on road signs or in menus don't make a whole lot of sense, try reading aloud to see if that helps. Spelling is often lost in translation, especially where there's no standard way for rendering the local alphabet into the Roman alphabet. This happens a lot in Thailand and as a result you'll find that what's written on the street sign is different from what's written in your guidebook, which again is different from what's printed on your map. Once you read them aloud, though, they sound the same and all will become clear.

In South America, it's Spanish or nothing (unless you're in Brazil and then it's Portuguese or nothing). If you didn't do Spanish at school but did do other languages you might find that with a little bit of French, or a smidgen of Italian, you can read basic information in Spanish. The vocabulary is fairly similar. Speaking it is a different matter, though – the words look the same but they're pronounced quite differently. This trips up even those who do know some Spanish – Latin American Spanish is different from Spanish Spanish. You know those spittle-inducing 'th's like in the word Barcelona (which when pronounced by a Spaniard as 'Barthelona' sounds to a British ear like someone's got a speech impediment)? Well, they don't exist in Latin Ameri-can Spanish. Instead, the same sound is pronounced 'ss'. The letter 'j' sounds like a 'k' when spoken and, even more confusingly, a double l, 'll', is pronounced like the 'j' in jam. Thus, in South America, the haughty-looking and noble llama is made to sound, to a European ear, like an abbreviated form of nightclothes.

When English isn't English

After leaving non-English speaking countries behind and landing in former colonies, you might assume that your language problems are over. Unfortunately that's not always the case. Sometimes even English isn't English; words mean something entirely different to what they mean in the mother tongue and there's potential for confusion – sometimes amusing, sometimes embarrassing. To save your blushes, here's a quick list of some of the ones to watch out for and what they really mean:

Great tramps: when used in New Zealand this refers not to famous vagrants or celebrated ladies of the night but in fact scenic walks over rugged terrain. The verb 'to tramp' in New Zealand-speak roughly translates to the English 'to hike'.

Thongs: in Sydney, you may see signs outside of bars boldly declaring NO THONGS. 'But, how do they know?' I hear you cry. Fortunately, you won't be walking over mirrors or facing an underwear inspection on the way in. 'Thongs' is, in fact, the Australian word for flip-flops. The

Kiwis call the same item 'jandals' (shortened from 'Japanese sandals', which is quite sensible, if not as evocative as the English).

To root: in Australia and New Zealand this means 'to enjoy vigorous sexual relations'. It's broadly equivalent to the English verb 'to roger'. I recommend that you do not announce to a crowded campsite that you've just spent hours rooting around in the back of the van for a camping stove.

Top shelf: if a Kiwi bloke asks you if you fancy some top shelf, don't slap him. He's not referring to pornographic magazines, instead he's asking you if you want a spirit. The correct response is something like: 'Vodka tonic, please'.

Pants: in Australia, New Zealand, Canada and America, 'pants' means 'trousers'. I know that you already know this, it's just that sometimes you momentarily forget when someone asks if they can borrow your pants. It's not as bad as it sounds.

All right: we English tend to use this as a greeting. We know that it just means 'How are you?' or 'You OK?' or even just 'Nice to see you'. Aussies, Kiwis and Americans don't get this. To them, you only ask if someone's all right if they look seriously rough. They might be a bit annoyed with you if you repeatedly use the phrase 'all right' in their presence.

Lost in translation

Sometimes, even when an English translation is provided, it might not be all that much help. If we can't even manage to understand other nations who are supposed to speak the same language as us, what hope have we got with everyone else? Menus are a fertile breeding ground for this kind of confusion. In Russia, I was offered 'meat wrapped in grape sheets', which while not entirely explanatory, did at least give me some idea of the likely ingredients. (After some lateral thinking, I was able to deduce that this meant 'stuffed vine leaves'.) The English menu in one Chinese eating establishment was completely beyond my powers of deduction, politely offering the following selection of dishes:

> The jumps up the wall stew
> The red bean wipes the tea drink
> Three kinds of colours complain the noodles
> Harbour key-ins the expensive of chips
> Sour and lousy inebriate to cheat the stew
> The rib of the juice comes to Holland

I suspect even Sherlock Holmes would be stumped by these. Call me unadventurous but in a country where fried chicken's feet are considered part of a normal breakfast and most meat dishes come with bones, skin and veins still attached, I wasn't prepared to take a guess and brave ordering any of these, so sadly, I'll never know what they were.

DOs and DON'Ts for surmounting language barriers and avoiding other cultural slip-ups

- DO learn to distinguish between the Ladies and the Gents and learn enough of the language to at least be able to say 'Thank you'.

- DO read something aloud if it doesn't make sense written down (although I concede that even that wouldn't have helped in the case of the Chinese menu).
- DON'T assume that just because Australians, Americans, New Zealanders and Canadians speak English, we're all speaking the same language. What they think you mean may not be what you actually mean.
- DO try to have at least a little Spanish if you want to go to South America. If you're really stuck, a bit of French and Italian together with some confidently Spanish-sounding waffle will go a long way. Failing that, speak Spanglish – English with a funny accent and putting an 'o' on the end of all the words.
- DON'T, under any circumstances, use the verb 'to root' in Australia. Instead simply say: 'I'm looking for . . .'
- DO be careful about asking colonial cousins if they're 'all right'.
- DO remember that in some places in the world pants means trousers, not underwear.
- DON'T assume that just because there's an English menu it'll be any easier to order your food.

TOP FIVE BRANDS THAT PROBABLY WON'T GO GLOBAL

Coming in at number five, it's the Kiwi lemon and spring water soft drink known as **L&P** (or Lemon and Paeroa – after the town it comes from). Proudly promoted as 'World Famous in New Zealand', it uses advertising slogans that are about as subtle as Prince Philip at a politically sensitive dinner. Spotted on a billboard in the centre of Auckland: 'L&P and fish and chips, goes together like sand and butt cracks'. Can't see that working in the middle of London.

At four, it's the Malaysian fast food chicken chain named after its founder, American country and western giant Kenny Rogers. Not a whole sentence in its original American English, it has an entirely different meaning in English English: I'm not sure many of us would fancy tucking into some **Kenny Rogers Roasters**.

Into the top three now, and at three it's **Pocari Sweat** drinking water, widely available throughout China. Anyone?

At two, narrowly missing out on the top spot, is the range of Indian men's underwear proudly advertised throughout the country as the number one best-seller. It might be over there but I suspect that European men would be less keen to sport the label **Bum Chums**.

And finally, coming in at number one, it's our highest new entry, from Peru . . . it's **Fanny Tuna**. Enough said.

Chapter Nine

SHOP TACTICS

I thought that might get your attention! If you're a serial shopper then there's a whole new world of browsing and buying for you to enjoy in the markets and malls of the world. There's so much out there that it's easy to get caught up in the excitement of the bargain hunt. Beware, however, the strange seduction of souvenir shopping – that compulsion that means you just have to have objects which are totally useless and look completely out of place once you get them back home. You will, in all likelihood, make some very ill-advised purchases on your travels, but that's all part of the fun. One day, when your travelling time is long behind you, you'll clear out a cupboard and unearth that cactus ornament sculpted from salt that you bought in Bolivia. In addition to wondering why on earth you thought it was a good idea to buy it in the first place, you'll smile and remember fondly the places you went and the people you met. In any case, any self-respecting backpacker would consider their round-the-world trip incomplete without bringing home a poncho, a soapstone model of a terracotta warrior, several carved wooden giraffes, a selection of garishly coloured and boldly patterned cushion covers and a small wooden frog that makes a croaking sound when you run a stick along its back.

I can tell you're eager to get out there and start spending. Just before you do, I'm going to be boring and mention a couple of words of caution: budget and backpack. Keep an eye on what you can afford to spend. You don't want to be eating nothing but two-minute noodles for three weeks in Month Four just because you purchased an excess of earrings in Australia. Also think of backpack space. Remember that whatever you buy, you have to carry – at least until you can send it home somehow (of which more in the next chapter). Don't do what my friend did and buy a huge woven blanket in Ecuador then have to lug it around the (rather warm) wilderness for the next two months.

There are, however, some amazing bargains out there, so don't miss out on those. To get the really good deals, check out the 'Recommended Buys' section of your guidebooks, which will give you some idea of where the best deals can be found and what items really are good value for money in each locale. Bangkok particularly is a shopper's paradise – and the tailoring there is amazing as well. If you're into your labels but don't have the cash to match, India can fill your wardrobe with passable fakes at prices that are more backpacker than Bond Street. And even when you haven't got any intention of actually buying anything, a visit to a local market passes some time and can be great fun – banter with the stallholders and check out some weird and wonderful wares. The Witches' Market in La Paz, for example, is a must see, although I seriously doubt that you'll want to purchase a dried llama foetus.

You're probably wondering why you need a chapter on shopping. After all, you're an expert, you practise your art every weekend. However, buying in a bustling market in Beijing isn't quite the same as buying in terribly polite oh-so-English shops where no one talks to you unless you ask a question and you can just wander about and have a look without any pressure at all. So, to enhance your overseas shopping experiences, here are a few things you might need to know.

STREET SELLERS

This is not a species that's fussy about its habitat. You'll encounter this breed almost everywhere – the Med, Africa, Asia, South America. Even when you're not in shopping mode they'll still be in your face: 'You wanna buy a watch?', 'CD, DVD?', 'Water? Cool drink?' Here's a rough example of how it goes: an earnest-looking Peruvian will approach, desperately trying to persuade you to buy a hat. The flaw in his plan, you think, is quite obvious. You're already wearing a hat, clearly you don't need another one. You gesture at your hat, smile, shake your head and move on. After twenty more minutes and twenty more Peruvians trying to sell you a hat, it's no longer amusing and is in fact quite irritating. It's very tempting at this point to dish out a generous portion of English sarcasm and rant at the street seller: 'Can't you see, I'm already wearing a hat? Why would I need another one? Of course, maybe you've noticed that I have another head I'm not presently aware of and you're trying to politely draw my attention to it.' Satisfying as this may be, effective it is not. South American pedlars don't have a very good grasp of English and they also have amazingly thick skin (maybe it's the altitude?). They'll patiently listen to your rant for a good few minutes, apparently convinced that you're admiring their goods in a loud and rather aggressive manner. When the message does eventually sink in and they realize that you have absolutely no intention of buying a second hat, they'll wander off disconsolately in search of another unsuspecting victim – but in the meantime you'll have wasted quite some time out of your day and wound yourself up. It's just not worth it. Instead, the best way to discourage these ridiculously optimistic street traders is a simple but firm *'No, gracias'*. You can even buy T-shirts with NO GRACIAS emblazoned on the front. Just might be a worthwhile investment.

Indian street sellers, on the other hand, require a slightly different tactic. They're more persistent. And they speak English. If you try to explain to them *why* you don't want to buy whatever it is they're trying to sell you, they'll reason with you, plead with you, say anything to keep you engaged in conversation – all in the hope that they'll wear you down eventually. And believe me, they really are persistent, even in the face of adversity. One auto rickshaw driver in Agra followed me at walking pace down the road for a full ten minutes AFTER I told him I was going to walk to the Internet café and therefore *didn't* require an auto rickshaw, chorusing: 'Excuse me . . . madam . . . auto rickshaw . . . hello?'

It doesn't feel right, but in the end it's easier just to ignore them altogether than to try to formulate a polite yet firm reply. No matter what you say to them they'll always have a comeback, so you'll be there forever. You just have to walk away. If the worst comes to the worst and you can't see any other way out, start looking round for somewhere with a toilet, pretend you've had a sudden attack of Delhi belly and run, clutching your stomach as you go.

With a bit of practice, extensive avoidance experience will start to tell. Once you've been running the street-seller gauntlet for a few weeks you'll realize that you're being accosted less. What's happened is that you've somehow developed a 'fuck off' face which kicks into action without prompting from you and which causes sellers to veer out of your path and pick on greener-looking companions instead. Keep that face. Summon it up at will just by thinking hard about how annoyed you were about being harassed on the streets of Cusco, or Delhi, or Shanghai, or wherever. It works on street sellers but it also comes in very handy at home for discouraging high-street charity collectors.

DOs and DON'Ts for dealing with street sellers

- DO invest in a NO GRACIAS T-shirt if you're in South America for any decent period of time, and wear it without mercy.
- DON'T assume that just because you clearly already own a hat/sunglasses/watch this will in any way suggest that you don't need another one.

- DO forget about English politeness – just ignore street sellers and walk off if they're not taking no for an answer.
- DON'T lose that 'fuck off' face, it's an investment – store it up to use again on people who hassle you on the high street at home.

HEY, BIG SPENDER!

If you've ever wondered what it might be like to be a millionaire, Zimbabwe should be on your list of places to visit. Now that Italy no longer has the lira, it's probably your best bet for somewhere where you can spend fifty thousand cash in just a few minutes. The locals will love you – tourists are their main (sometimes only) source of income, and Victoria Falls is worth seeing as well.

To add to the feeling of reckless abandon, change up your money on the black market – the exchange rate is likely to be something close to ten times better than the government's published rate, so even if you get given a few fake notes, they're not worth that much anyway.

There's just one thing to watch out for: the notes have an expiry date printed on them, so it's not worth keeping them. Instead, get on out there and spend, spend, spend. What a great excuse to go shopping.

THE GAME OF THE HAGGLE

Learning to avoid street traders is one thing, but what if you do actually want to buy something? That'll mean having a close look at the goods and therefore demonstrating that you're interested – which will immediately put you on the receiving end of even more persuasive chat from the stallholder. If you like what you see, you'll then have to engage in the actual act of purchasing. Unfortunately, it's not like at home where you look at the price, decide whether you're prepared to pay it and, if you are, hand the money over in exchange for the goods. In the markets of the world, there are no price tags. Instead, haggling is the name of the shopping game.

I don't know about you, but I'm not a comfortable haggler. It doesn't sit well with the British psyche. We're reserved and we're polite, we don't like to embarrass ourselves and we don't like to upset anyone else. With haggling, though, it's necessary to be borderline insulting, perhaps even actively rude – one haggling tactic is to walk away while the trader is still mid-sentence if you're really trying to get them to drop their price. The other challenging thing about the haggle is that you have to initiate it, which means you have to think of a starting price, balancing the risk of over-offering with the danger of going so low that you offend. Don't worry, like the 'fuck off' face, it gets better with practice.

My early experiments with haggling (during the annual

two-week holiday) weren't in the least bit successful. I'm still haunted by the memory of a terrible shopping trip in Egypt when I really wanted to buy a top, but obviously couldn't do so without trying it on. Doing that demonstrated that a) it didn't suit me, and b) it wasn't very well made. There was no way I was buying it, but the stallholder wasn't having any of it when I tried to return it to him or place it back on his stall. Instead he chose to believe that I was bargaining very hard to get it. This episode ended with an agonizing, loud and very public scene (much to my very British embarrassment) which was concluded only when I dropped the garment in question on the floor and walked away, followed by a volley of insults. Cringing, I exited the market immediately and abandoned all hope of going shopping that day. I was embarrassed and left feeling that it was all my fault. It put me right off haggling for a while, but I got back into it. If you happen to have a bad experience, try not to worry about it, just walk away and try again somewhere else.

Fortunately for me (and for you), the South American and Asian haggling experience is much more civilized and far less threatening than the Egyptian. Once you get into it, you'll find that it's actually quite good fun. Practise a little bit first on things that you'd like to buy, but only if they're at the right price. Save the things that you really want until you've got a bit of experience behind you. Remember to smile and be polite, but also to have a clear idea in your head of how much you are prepared to pay for the item.

Smiling and politeness are particularly critical to the

242

success of the haggle in Asia. The concept of 'face' is cultur-
ally huge there (as in your stallholder can't be seen to 'lose
face'), so ask, rather than demand. Preface price offers with
phrases like 'Would it be possible for . . .' or 'Could you do
it for . . ', as you will make it seem like the stallholder is
doing you a favour. If you can manage to learn a little of the
language, conducting the negotiations, or even part of
them, in the native tongue will mean that you'll almost
always be treated with more respect and get better prices.
Above all, remember that haggling is a game – relax, enjoy
it and be prepared to lose sometimes.

The typical haggle goes something like this:

Step 1: Ask the price or make an offer.

Step 2: The stallholder gives you an optimistically inflat-
ed price, recognizing that that's not where you'll end up.

Step 3: Make a counter-offer of a ridiculously low price.
A useful guideline for this is to offer somewhere between
half and two thirds of the stallholder's original price.

Step 4: Listen to the stallholder make a second offer,
normally somewhere in the middle of their original price
and your ridiculously low counter-offer.

Step 5: Look doubtful, examine the item again and look
thoughtful (you're meant to convey the impression that
you're thinking about how much you want it and whether
it's worth paying that for it. In reality, of course, you're
not thinking anything of the sort since you've decided
all that before you asked the price in the first place. But in
this game, it's very important to look like you can be persuaded).

243

Step 6: If you stretch Step 5 out for long enough, the stallholder will launch into a spiel about how you're driving a hard bargain, how he has fifteen children at home to feed and how you're robbing him. Your role is to listen to this without comment.

Step 7: Repeat your offer at about the same level as in Step 4.

Step 8: Continue with offer and counter-offer until eventually agreeing on a figure. Hand over the money, smile and say thank you. Leave with your purchase and a sense of achievement.

If you really want to push the point (and don't mind taking a risk that you might end up not buying the item), walk away at Step 8. If your offer had in fact been reasonable and the stallholder is just trying to see how far he can push you, he'll suddenly and miraculously decide to accept your price, even though he'll tell you that it's killing him to do so and his children won't eat for a week if he sells everything at that price. If, on the other hand, you walk away and he doesn't come after you then that's a safe bet that your offer was ridiculously low. You won't be buying that particular item from him. However, you'll probably find another stall a bit further along selling essentially the same thing, so you can try again, having effectively done your research regarding appropriate pricing during the first haggle. If you can't get anyone to agree to what you want to pay then clearly you're pitching it way too low. You need to decide if you're prepared to pay more (which generally depends on how much you want it) and if you are, you'll have to go back and try again. If you do have to go back, your bargaining position is much weakened second time around. The stallholder knows that you *really* want whatever it is they're selling, so you'll pretty much have to agree to whatever price they ask for.

After a bit of practice, you'll be haggling away like a native. The 'savings' you make by talking the price down won't be huge but you'll be playing the game, and the Game of the Haggle is one of those sports where it's the taking part that counts, not how much you win. There are opportunities to drive some really good deals, but in the main, you're in it for the experience, not for the money. When totting up your savings, always think in local currency; don't convert it back to pounds or you'll be disappointed. After extensive bargaining at the enormous market in Pisaq, Peru, I returned to the bus exhilarated about the massive savings I'd managed to make – until I calculated that across my six purchases I'd saved myself the princely sum of £1.85p.

DOs and DON'Ts for the Game of the Haggle

- DO smile and be polite (especially in Asia).
- DO know what the maximum you're prepared to pay for the item is before you start out.
- DON'T necessarily expect to make huge savings.
- DO enter into the spirit of things when haggling for something you want to buy. It's the game that matters, not the fact that you're arguing over 23p.

245

- DO be prepared to walk away if you can't get the price you want – treat it as research.
- DO remember that if you repeatedly can't get what you want at the price you want to pay, then you're probably being too stingy.
- DO remember that taking part is more important than winning.

THE TROUBLE WITH ATMS

I know we call them cash points or cash machines at home. The rest of the world calls them ATMs. Incidentally, the rest of the world mispronounces the word 'hostel' as well. For the first few weeks of your trip other travellers will laugh at you for saying cash point or 'hostul', so you'll change it and start saying ATM and 'hosTEL'. Then you'll come home and get funny looks for saying ATM instead of cash point and 'hosTEL' instead of 'hostul'. It's just one of those things. You'll get used to it.

Anyway, back to the point. Whatever you call it, frequent visits to an ATM are a necessary evil of long-term travelling. Trying to start out with enough cash to see you through your whole trip is just not possible. Travellers' cheques are an option if you're travelling in Europe, North America, Australia and New Zealand (and they're certainly more secure than carrying cash), but outside of that the procedure for changing them into local currency is usually ridiculously complex and time-consuming, even if you can find an opportunity to try it. Which is not always easy. Firstly there are not many places that will take travellers' cheques, and then those places that do take them have opening hours that are so illogical, limited and restrictive that they might as well be governed by the phases of the moon. Unfortunately, the places where it's tough to cash up travellers' cheques such as South America and parts of Asia also tend to be the countries where there's often a higher fraud risk associated with using your credit card, or where cards simply aren't accepted, so you'll need heaps of ordinary, old-fashioned cash. As a result, ATMs will become very familiar to you.

After you've been travelling for a while, you'll start to wonder why on earth you ever got into a panic about changing money up into local currency before going on holiday. There's an ATM at almost every airport in the world so in most cases you can simply withdraw some cash when you arrive. Yes, you might get charged a withdrawal fee but it's usually comparable to the fee you'd pay to change the currency at home (unless you can find a no-fees foreign exchange deal, or can get a bank account which doesn't charge for overseas withdrawals). Whenever you do get cash out, you'll want to get a fair amount to avoid paying multiple withdrawal fees. Try not to have too much more cash than is covered by your travel insurance, though – you won't be able to claim more than that back if gets stolen.

Getting cash out of machines on the street can be a bit scary – you might be worried about card fraud or someone grabbing your purse just after they've watched you fill it with lots of lovely notes. The risks are probably no higher than at home, but risks there are. To minimize them, try to use machines inside buildings where possible, always cover the keypad when you enter your PIN and try to go in pairs if you can so you've got someone to watch your back. You know the scams to look out for – they don't change just because you're in a different country. If the machine appears not to be working, for example, just remove your card and walk away. Don't get distracted by any passing stranger who comes to 'help'. When you do get cash out of a machine, put it somewhere safe and preferably secure immediately – don't wander away from the machine with it still in your hand. Split the wad up as well – put some in your purse or your bag and some somewhere else (like in your bra).

The other problem with ATMs is that they work on the basis of an international Sod's Law which dictates that in the countries where you need small denomination notes (to avoid repeating scenes similar to the Bolivian café proprietor's money-changing dash on a daily basis), the ATMs will give you very large denomination notes that you'll then struggle to spend. Conversely, in countries like New Zealand and Australia where large denomination notes don't cause a problem, ATMs will give you lots of small denomination notes so your purse will be bulging and it'll be obvious to everyone that you're carrying quite a lot of cash. There's not a lot you can do about it really, it's just one of those travelling things. You'll just get used to apologizing for your money because it's too big and you'll arrive somewhere like Australia and receive many strange looks in shops and restaurants when you apologize profusely for being forced to hand over such an unreasonable amount of money as a $20 note.

DOs and DON'Ts for using ATMs

- DO accept that it's just one of those facts of life that ATMs will never give you notes in denominations that will be practical for whatever country you're in at the time. It adds to the challenge and keeps things interesting.
- DON'T stress about getting your currency before you get to where you're going – airports generally do have ATMs.
- DO try to get an account which doesn't charge you for cash withdrawals abroad – you'll need to organize this some time in advance of leaving home.
- DON'T accept the assistance of strangers if you're struggling to get the machine to work – just retrieve your card and walk away.
- DON'T apologize for your money when you're in the Antipodes.

HOW TO BUY TOOTHPASTE IN ARGENTINA

You might be wondering why it's necessary for me to provide you with an entire section on this one action, which, on the face of it, you may assume to be a basic task. Don't be fooled. It's not as easy as simply going into the supermarket and selecting something that looks like it might be toothpaste from the shelf. For a start, most Argentinian supermarkets don't sell toiletries and cosmetics, so you have to go to the pharmacy instead. It's not until you get to the pharmacy that you realize why this might be a problem. Treat this story like a case study – you can apply the lessons it teaches to any tricky shopping trip, anywhere in the world.

Once you get to your Argentinian pharmacy, you could be forgiven for thinking that it was designed solely for the purpose of thwarting foreigners. Not for Argentina the tried-and-tested, understood-the-world-over system of displaying goods for customers to browse among, consider, compare, make a choice and take to the till to make payment. Oh no. That would clearly be far too easy. Instead, in Argentina, toothpastes, deodorants, cough medicines, headache tablets and the like are treated as priceless jewels. They're kept under lock and key in glass display cabinets behind counters patrolled by assistants who look like nothing so much as caricatures of public-school draconian disciplinarians. It doesn't encourage browsing.

In order to actually make a purchase, a lengthy and torturous procedure has to be completed. Firstly, it is necessary to communicate your desire for the toothpaste to the formidably brooding presence behind the counter. Then, you are required to complete a ritual even more bizarre and drawn out in order to pay for and collect it.

If you haven't got a phrase book or a decent Spanish accent, the first part of the transaction – communicating which item you need – tends to involve an elaborate pan-tomime of pointing and miming which, after many strange and puzzled looks, will eventually result in the dawning of comprehension. At that point, you will be presented with a ticket stating what it is that you wish to purchase (i.e. the toothpaste). There will then be a short interlude during which the shop assistants will try to explain to you (in Spanish) what happens next. When this fails, there will then be a period of miming, pointing and hand-waving by the assistants which you will eventually realize directs you around the shop to another counter, where you will have to hand over your little ticket, pay for your toothpaste and collect a receipt. Notice, at this point, that I have not yet suggested that you will actually be in possession of the toothpaste itself. Further pointing, miming and hand-waving will direct you to yet another counter, at which your toothpaste will finally be retrieved from its tiny glass tomb. You will watch in astonishment as it is passed on to the fourth and, thankfully, final counter, where it will be placed in a bag and ceremoniously presented to you.

I have no idea why this extended operation is required in order to purchase toiletries. I can only assume that the country either aims for full employment by taking on at least three times as many staff as are actually necessary to facilitate the purchase of these items and inventing jobs for them to do; or that there is a seriously high risk of toiletry theft, requiring the combined protection of vigilant and eagle-eyed staff together with lockable storage cabinets.

A quick tip for making the initial communication

process easier wherever you may be on your travels – make sure you're proficient in the international language of MAP (Mime and Point). You should also practise your mime before you get to the shop to avoid either getting stage fright or to prevent your mind going blank at the critical moment, and remember that most other countries, Argentina included, don't get *Give Us a Clue*. Actions like those that correspond with 'Three words . . . first word, two syllables . . .' mean nothing. Just don't use them; they'll make things more difficult than they already are. If you put your mind to it, toothpaste is relatively easy to mime. You need to enact holding the brush, squeezing the tube out, then brushing your teeth. There's occasionally a degree of confusion as to whether you're trying to indicate the brush or the paste, but you can usually sort that out. Alternatively, you can buy little books which are full of pictures of things you might want to buy so you can take those along to a shop or a restaurant and simply point at what you want. It's nowhere near as much fun though.

If you don't have a book full of pictures, the tactic of mime is extremely useful, no matter where in the world you are, to get what you want in any given shop when you don't speak the language. The bad news is that some mimes are much easier to perform than others. When I caught a heavy cold, I had some success with my brief pantomime of coughing and pretending to blow my nose, pointing to my head and groaning. After some puzzled looks, I did eventually get some decongestant tablets. The modest limits of my acting talents unfortunately didn't extend to a medicated hot lemon drink, which would have been extra soothing, but the decongestant tablets did the job adequately enough. If you think your miming talents may similarly stumble over a hot lemon drink, make sure you pack some into your first-aid kit before you leave home.

The requirement to mime your shopping list and the sheer number of people you have to deal with during an Argentinian toothpaste-purchasing experience should act as a warning to you about the importance of packing properly before you leave home. I for one was extremely grateful that I'd packed what turned out to be an optimistically large supply of condoms. That's one mime I definitely don't fancy attempting in an Argentinian chemist's shop.

DOs and DON'Ts of buying toothpaste in Argentina, and tips for other random shopping expeditions

* DO try the easy route first – if you can get it in the supermarket, that's probably going to be the best option.
* DON'T despair in any situation where you don't speak the language – there is always mime.
* DO think through and practise your mime before you get to the shop, so that at least one of you knows what you're doing.
* DO try not to run out of toothpaste in Argentina.
* DON'T forget to pack the condoms.

Chapter Ten

BACKPACKER PHONE HOME – AND OTHER METHODS OF COMMUNICATION

While you're away, you'll no doubt want to keep in touch with your friends and family back home. You're lucky – with the Internet, mobile phones and digital cameras it's a LOT easier to stay in touch than it used to be. I have friends who backpacked a long time before technology was much help – they tell tales of backpacks full of undeveloped film, agonizing over whether it was safer to keep carrying it and risk losing the backpack, or post it home and risk it getting lost in the post. They also tell of visits to random post offices to check the poste restante mail just in case there was something for them. Now, with email, text and instant messaging, you can be in touch with home regularly and get almost instantaneous replies – you don't even need to know what poste restante means any more.

Even if travelling, to you, means leaving it all behind and not worrying about the real world, you will have to phone home at some point because, trust me, your mum will worry if she doesn't hear your voice occasionally. She'll tell you that email just isn't the same. You might also want to send email updates to your friends (principally to make them jealous), do a blog, or share your photos. All of that will mean you'll need regular Internet access. So, in this chapter, I'll give you a low-down on the basics of staying in touch, take you on a brief tour of the post offices of the world (not for the poste restante but because if you're a serial shopper you'll have to send your purchases home somehow) and share some of my more bizarre experiences of international cyberspace.

THE BASICS

Using the phone

You'll almost certainly be planning to take your mobile with you. Check with your phone company before you leave home for overseas accessibility and costs so you know what countries your phone will theoretically work in, and so you don't get a shock when the bill arrives. Often, making and receiving international calls on a mobile is expensive, so you might want to save it for emergencies or just to send texts. It's quite handy when you realize you've just forgotten your best mate's birthday. Even if you haven't sent a card, she won't feel quite so unloved if you do manage to send a quick text on the day.

If you're going to be staying in one country for a couple of months or longer it might be worth investing in a local SIM so you can make calls and text other local mobiles more cheaply. Remember that if you're abroad using your home SIM to text friends in the same country as you, you'll still be charged international rates regardless of whether they're on a home or a foreign SIM. Also, be aware that any free text or call time packages you have at home often don't operate elsewhere, so be prepared to be charged every time you use your phone.

No matter where you are in the world, mobile phone reception can be a bit unreliable, so if you're going out into the back of beyond, don't rely on your mobile phone for emergencies. In the Australian outback, for example, nothing but special satellite phones work and if you break down it could literally be days before anyone comes by to help you out. If you are going out into the sticks, make plans such as hiring a suitable phone if necessary before you go to ensure you can call for help if something does go wrong. Charging your phone might also prove challenging at times, especially if you're spending a fair amount of time camping or staying in places where you don't have easy access to mains electricity. Be warned – this doesn't just mean Africa; some of the more out-of-the-way parts of New Zealand and Australia aren't on the grid either. If you think lack of electricity is going to be a problem for you, investigate options for wind-up or solar chargers. They're generally not too big so can be carried relatively easily if you are going to be off the beaten track. Check out travel websites to buy them if required.

Unless you've got a really good international calling deal on your mobile, a landline is probably going to work out cheaper for things like phoning your nan on her birthday or speaking to your mum – especially when she insists on telling you all the gossip about someone you went to primary school with but haven't spoken to for ten years just because she saw their mum in town the other day. NB – mums tend not to understand that the fact that you're in Thailand means that a) that's not really relevant information, b) you wouldn't really be that fussed about it even if you were at home, c) you're paying for this call, and d) every minute you spend on the phone is a minute less on the beach. For these tedious but necessary calls, international phone cards are a good option. They work by getting you to dial a local access number and put in the PIN code from the card, then they let you dial internationally for an impressively cheap per-minute rate. You can use them from telephone boxes (after putting a coin in to pay for the initial local call) but also from normal home phones, so if you're couch surfing at friends' or relatives' you can make calls from there without feeling guilty about running up a huge bill. Your guidebooks should be able to give you the low-down on which ones are the best locally and where to buy them from. If not, a newsagent is usually a good starting point.

If you can't spot any public phone boxes, look instead for telephone offices. They're like little shops full of small cabins, usually containing a telephone and a display so you can see how long you've been on the call and how much it's costing you. You pay for the call at the end. Sometimes these offices are combined with Internet cafés. As well as generally being cheaper to use than payphones, telephone offices and international calling cards mean that you don't have to put your back out by carrying around seven tonnes of small change.

Another option for making cheap, or even free, calls is to use Internet calling packages such as Skype. If you're travelling with your laptop this is especially easy as you can dial up anywhere you can find wireless access. If not, some Internet cafés have packages installed and can provide headsets. Just remember that although the headphones mean that only you can hear the person you're talking to, everyone else in the room can hear your end of the conversation. And they will listen in, so this is not the time to engage in phone sex – instant messenger is a far better option.

Using the Internet

Internet access is often easier to find than you might expect it to be – even in random corners of the world. In fact out of all the places I've visited, it was hardest to track down an Internet café in New York city. I suspect this is because too many of the locals have access at home so there isn't the demand. On the other hand, in India, in Bolivia, in Kenya, even in Zimbabwe – places where you might expect to struggle to find anything so advanced as a computer with an Internet connection – there were Internet cafés virtually everywhere you looked. Admittedly, speed was not always of the essence. In fact sometimes connections were so slow it felt like it would be quicker to use carrier pigeon, but Internet access it was. How is it that these countries have failed to develop a sewage system that can cope with toilet paper, yet still manage to have Internet cafés in even the tiniest of towns?

Most of the time (except perhaps in New York) the real trick is not in tracking down some Internet access, but in tracking down cheap Internet access. Less money on the Internet means more money on wine, so you don't want to pay more than you have to. Many hostels will offer Internet access, which is definitely convenient – but it may not necessarily be the best value. Put that bargain-hunting head on and shop around a bit to see what rates are on offer elsewhere. Look for Internet cafés, but also other places that might have one or two terminals with access at reasonable rates – mini marts, newsagents, cafés, video shops, community centres or even the local library.

If you're going predominantly to places like North America, Australia or New Zealand and you have a wi-fi enabled laptop, it might pay to take it with you. Internet access in hostels is often cheaper, or even free, with your own laptop, or you can grab a coffee and log on. New York may not have had any Internet cafés, but it did have a fair few wi-fi spots. Backpacker insurance policies don't normally cover things like laptops so you'll need to insure it separately if you're going to take it.

Blogging and photo sharing

This is a great way to keep family and friends in touch with your travels, and it means you can show off all the fab beaches you're chilling on and the gorgeous guys you're meeting. There are lots of blog sites out there, including many that specialize in travel, and some are free to post on. A quick Google search should find you a selection to check out. Similarly with photo-sharing sites – there are many to choose from, and what better way to make your friends jealous? Uploading your photos also acts as a back-up just in case something happens to your camera or your memory card. And do make sure you back up. I know someone who stored a whole gap year's worth of photos on his iPod, only for it to crash and lose the lot. He didn't back them up anywhere else. Your photos of your trip are your memories and losing them is a bit like finding out that your mum has mistakenly recycled your love letters from your first boyfriend. Do pack your USB cable so that you can download easily from your camera. The alternative is a footsore and perpetual mission to find Internet cafés with memory card readers.

DOs and DON'Ts of keeping in touch

- DO shop around for the best deal on Internet time – this may not be found at your hostel.
- DO check out your guidebooks for tips on how to phone home cheaply.
- DO phone your mum occasionally – she worries.
- DON'T rely on your mobile phone for emergencies if you're going somewhere a bit off the beaten track.
- DO consider buying a local SIM if you're going to be in one country for any length of time.
- DO make sure you insure your laptop if you're going to take it with you.
- DO back up your photos just in case disaster strikes.
- DO understand that it will probably be easier to find

an Internet café in a Third World country than in most First World ones – just don't expect the connection speed to be anything other than hair-tearingly slow.

THE CONFUSIONS OF
INTERNATIONAL CYBERSPACE

Ease of access, price, the quality of equipment and speed of connection are the variables you might expect to be juggling when using alien Internet. What you might not expect is any kind of language barrier, unusual keyboard layouts or having to prove you are who you say you are before being allowed into the Net café. With travelling, however, it's often the things you thought would be no problem at all which surprise you. So, here's a quick outline of some of the more unusual problems you might face and some ideas for getting around them.

Keyboard layout

I'll admit, it's not something you give much thought to but, had I been asked, I probably would have said that a computer keyboard would be the same the world over. Sounds logical, doesn't it? They're manufactured in huge factories and shipped all round the globe, surely they wouldn't bother changing the layout depending on which country they're producing for. Would they? Apparently, they do.

This wouldn't be too much of a problem if the keys that were changed were ones you didn't use all that often. However, the key that is most often relocated is the @ key. Which is a problem as you use @ a lot – logging into your email, addressing email, logging into Facebook, logging into pretty much anything . . . You probably know where the @ key is on an English keyboard without thinking about it too much. It's just along from the L, next to the semicolon. Suddenly, when you're travelling, every time you try to use your email address to log in to a website it doesn't work. It takes a while to twig that the reason for this is that pretty much everywhere else in the world, the @ symbol is above the 2 key. That is, unless you end up in a Net café which has really old equipment and doesn't even have an @ key on the keyboard. There is a way to get an @ but it requires the pressing of a bizarre and apparently random sequence of three keys in unison. To make things even more confusing, the sequence is different in different Internet cafés so you can't even memorize the combination. If you can't see an @ on the keyboard, look for a small sign either stuck to the computer itself or posted on a nearby wall to indicate what you need to press to make it work. Alternatively, if you get completely stuck with this you could always open Word, insert symbol, find the @, then copy and paste it to wherever you need it, assuming that Word isn't also talking to you in a different language!

If you're visiting South America (or, presumably, Spain) you're in for even more fun. As there are more letters in the Spanish alphabet than there are in the English alphabet, some computers are set up so that these extra letters take the place of some of the punctuation keys. The problem is that the actual keys on the keyboard don't show this, so you'll be happily pressing a normal, ordinary, everyday key (maybe something like the comma) and wondering why the spell checker is going crazy and your page is so covered in red marks that it looks more like your Year Eight maths homework than your email to your best mate about your latest conquest. What's happening is that each time you think you're selecting a comma, you're actually getting some random Spanish letter with an accent over it. And they don't do it consistently, so there aren't even any rules you can learn. Why they can't replace a single, little-used key – like backslash, maybe – I don't know. But they don't. That would be far too easy.

Sometimes, just to add to the fun, several keys will be reprogrammed. If this happens, the only way to sort it out is to engage in miniature-scale keyboard orienteering – without a map. Trial and error is the way to go – hit the key purporting to be the key that you want. If it doesn't produce the symbol you're expecting it to, search for the key displaying the symbol that it did produce. Try that key to see what that offers – sometimes you'll find that two keys have simply been swapped over for no apparent reason. If that doesn't work, look for the key displaying the symbol that the second key produced and try that one, and so on, continuing to follow the chain backwards and forwards across the keyboard until you find the symbol or letter that you actually want.

CHINESE CHECKERS

If you need to use the Internet in China, be prepared to go through a vetting system which is the cyberspace equivalent of the stringent security checks in a paranoid American airport. It is indeed as involved and bureaucratic as you may expect for a communist country. In order to be allowed anywhere near an Internet terminal, you'll first have to go through an extensive rigmarole involving production, inspection and copying of your passport, having your photo taken and filling out a form which will want to know everything there is to know about you, including your star sign. In addition, this will probably be another one of those instances, like buying toothpaste in Argentina, when you'll have to complete the entire operation while communicating solely through the means of MAP (Mime And Point). If you've left your passport in your hotel, don't even bother going anywhere near a Net café until you've gone back to collect it.

Once you've negotiated this ridiculous initiation of proving everything there is to prove about who you are excepting what size knickers you wear, and actually got onto the Internet, your access problems still may not be over as you might find you struggle to access some of the sites you want. If you hunt hard enough, you'll also find some interesting inconsistencies in Chinese cyberspace. Try typing the words 'Tiananmen Square' into Google in China, just to see what happens. You'll get lots of references to the Gate of Heavenly Peace but no mention at all of the 1989 massacre – which will be the first result you'll get anywhere else in the world. At the time of my visit (pre-Olympics), the BBC website was banned, yet, perplexingly, the *Sun*'s website was not. I can only conclude that the Chinese authorities felt that the *Sun* provides more balanced news coverage than the BBC.

Language barriers

Much as I erroneously assumed keyboard layouts would be the same the world over, I also assumed that the international language for everything Internet would be English. I was wrong on that, too. Most strange it is to log in to instant messaging in Argentina and find it conducting itself in Spanish. Trying to read the menus was useless, so starting a conversation was out. Instead, logging on and hoping someone else started talking was the best policy. Replying is pretty straightforward. It is nevertheless a little distracting to have all the signposting headings in Spanish rather than English. For example, instead of reading 'Dave says:' it reads 'Dave diz:'. Learn a lesson here – if there's a program or website you think you'll want to use while you're away, try memorizing the menu layout before you leave home to avoid this particular problem.

DOs and DON'Ts of avoiding cyberspace confusions

- DO remember that all keyboards are not created equal. Don't assume that the keys will either be the same as they are at home or that what it says on the key will be what it actually produces on the page.

Treat a foreign keyboard as virgin territory, to be explored and experimented with.

- DON'T get frustrated by repeatedly getting a message saying your login and/or password isn't correct when you know you've typed it right. Check that you've got the @ key instead of some other random punctuation.
- DO memorize the positioning of basic functionality on menus of applications you're particularly fond of, in case you need to use them in a different language later on.
- DO approach Chinese Internet cafés with your passport, some creative mime and a great deal of patience.

GOING POSTAL

I know snail mail is so last century, but there just might be times when you do actually need to post something. OK, so you're not likely to sit down and write a letter, but people like your grandparents who may not have email will be chuffed as anything to get a postcard. Also, if you really want to impress the people at home, send birthday cards to your close family and friends from abroad. They'll be amazed that you remembered and were organized enough to get it posted in time. In fact, they might be so stunned that they'll overlook the fact that you didn't get them a present. The time when the post office is most useful, though, is when you've overindulged in feeding your shopping habit and you just can't carry any more. Posting it home might be cheaper than paying excess baggage and it's certainly easier on your back.

Unfortunately, a degree of patience is required to negotiate the cavernous interiors and mysterious queuing systems of post offices the world over, as they seem to be the very bastions of the bureaucratic dinosaur. If you're wanting to dispatch a parcel, allow yourself plenty of time. A visit to the post office is an experience in itself. It could be as frustrating as meeting the new, seriously fit guy from accounts at the exact same moment as your colleague points out loudly that you've got a huge ladder in your tights; or it could be as smooth and satisfying as a recently waxed bikini line. Keep smiling, and remember that either you're sending something to your nearest and dearest (which will make them happy) or you're freeing up backpack space so you can do more shopping. Both of these are good things to be doing.

A trip to the post office

To find the post office and find out what services it's likely to offer, either consult your guidebook or ask at your hostel. That's the easy bit. Once you've got there, in addition to a good dose of patience, you might also benefit from a degree of guesswork, judicious use of your phrase book and some bold trial-and-error experimentation. Sometimes a visit to the post office takes half a day, so don't try to do this on the way to somewhere else. Set aside time for a post office trip. Treat it as a cultural experience.

A PARCEL FROM INDIA

By the end of my month-long stay in India it is fair to say that my expectations of the country's infrastructure were rather low. As a result, I was somewhat reluctant to trust anything to the Indian postal system, but if there's one thing about India, it's that it's cheap. I had done a lot of shopping. Some of it had to go as the zips on the backpack were literally about to burst.

On arrival at the main post office in Delhi, I was pleasantly surprised to find a sign outside proudly advertising a Parcel Packaging Department. Capital letters included – it was a bold, confident and professional-looking sign. I began to feel that maybe I had done the Indian postal system an injustice. Maybe, I started to think, it's the one organization which employs the only efficient people in the country. Not for long. Inside, I discovered that the Parcel Packaging Department was one man sat in a darkened corner of the post office surrounded by a heap of cardboard boxes and a pile of oddly shaped pieces of calico.

I joined the semicircle of bewildered-looking travellers surrounding the man and simply watched, fascinated. The parcel packaging process went something like this. Man takes someone's items. Man searches through pile of cardboard boxes (all bearing the brand names of various food items and clearly filched from the local supermarket). Man selects cardboard piece that looks to be roughly the right size. Man piles up all items on cardboard and cuts it to size. Man removes items from cardboard, wraps them in newspaper and replaces them on the cardboard. Man folds cardboard around newspaper parcel. Man fixes cardboard in place with yards and yards of brown parcel tape. Man selects a piece of the calico. Man cuts calico to size. Man wraps calico around cardboard enclosing newspaper-wrapped parcel. Man turns over a neat seam around each edge. Man sews entire parcel into a small calico bag. Man melts some wax, drops it in small blobs onto seams of parcel and stamps with seal. Man presents parcel and marker pen back to sender. Sender writes address on front of parcel. Sender departs Parcel Packaging Department to enter queue. It was like pass the parcel in reverse. I kept expecting the man to slip a handful of sweets in between each layer.

This performance did **not** increase my confidence in the Indian postal system. However, I patiently waited until it was deemed to be my turn to have my parcels wrapped. I then had to queue to purchase stamps for them, then queue to stick the stamps on, with glue pots reminiscent of my primary school days – India has apparently chosen not to bother with the convenience and innovation of the pre-gummed style of stamp used in the rest of the world. I then queued again to get to hand over my very securely wrapped parcels. By this point I was thinking that they'd never see the light of day again. I was wrong – they arrived home in a shorter time than anything else I sent all year. They didn't get opened very quickly, though – my Mum felt it necessary to take numerous photos of them and to cart them off to my grandparents' (still wrapped) so that they could see what a parcel from India looked like.

If you want your parcel to arrive at its destination in anything that might be considered a normal time period, wait until you're in a major town before posting. That might mean waiting three weeks, but if you leave a parcel at a village post office it'll have to be transferred to the main town before it gets dispatched overseas and three weeks is probably the quickest that would happen. In a worst case scenario it could be months. Unfortunately this means that if you want to send a gift home to arrive in time for a specific occasion, for example a birthday, it's a bit like doing the laundry. You have to plan the purchase, packaging and posting of the parcel in conjunction with your itinerary.

Finding the right queue

Finding the right counter for sending parcels abroad is your next challenge, after locating the post office. Unlike at home, in very large post offices every counter does not deal with every circumstance. To confuse the issue even further, there might be a deli-counter-style ticketing arrangement in operation, which may be segregated by activity. When you first arrive, take a good look around, looking especially for signs above the counters explaining what they do. Check out the number and location of any ticket dispensers and take the time to identify the correct ticketing machine for the queue you need. Only then take a number and wait your turn. It's worth investing a few minutes now to figure out the system and get the right queue rather than waiting in the wrong one for half an hour as the lady in front of you draws out her pension in two-pence pieces. Occasionally, if you're really lucky, there might be a sign in English at the entrance explaining how the system works, so have a look for that. It'll save you a lot of time.

Parcels

To wrap, or not to wrap? This is a bit of a vexed question. Unfortunately, the answer largely depends on where you are and what you're posting. Generally, it's probably easier to take your parcels to the post office unwrapped and get it sorted out there, but sometimes you'll have to wrap your parcels before you go, because the post office doesn't sell stationery. South America is like this, but there's generally an enterprising man outside selling envelopes and glue, so all is not lost. Most other places do seem to sell stationery in their post offices so it's easiest to get it all sorted out in the one place. If there happens to be an actual parcel packaging department, even though they charge a modest fee it's much easier to get them to do it for you. The alternative is spending ages trying to hunt out a stationer's, pointing and miming your way through your shopping list (envelope, bubble wrap, sticky tape) and, since you're unlikely to bother with having full-size scissors in your backpack, then having to cut the sticky tape with nail scissors. If you do wrap your parcel before getting to the post office it's best to leave it unsealed in case the counter clerk needs to inspect the contents for customs purposes. Take some sticky tape with you to seal your parcel once it's been solemnly declared (and possibly even rubber-stamped) as fit for posting, as the post office may not have any.

Be careful what you choose to post. If it's breakable, make sure it's well padded, and if it's valuable, either don't post it or consider paying extra for insurance. Your travel insurance is unlikely to cover things you've entrusted to a foreign postal system. If you are going to chance posting something valuable you need to do it when you first arrive somewhere rather than just as you're leaving, as if there is a problem, you'll need to be on hand to hassle people until they sort it out.

DOs and DON'Ts for pain-free parcel posting

- DO allow yourself a substantial amount of time to figure out the system, get your parcels wrapped and approved, queue up and eventually complete your transaction. Forget sightseeing; posting parcels home from random, far-flung locations is a backpacker rite of passage in itself.

- DO plan ahead if you want something to arrive in time for a particular date (like a birthday) – and don't post anything from rural post offices if you can possibly avoid it.

- DON'T assume that every counter will do everything. It's a bit like buying toothpaste in Argentina – every one of the counter clerks has their own little part to play in the grand scheme of things, and although the logic of it will probably elude you, you can do nothing but go along with it.

- DO post purchases home regularly to make more backpack space available for future shopping.

Chapter Eleven
THAT'S ENTERTAINMENT

In between going on your actual journeys, bargain hunting, kitchen warfare, laundry experiments, sleep interruption and chatting to strangers, you might wonder when you're going to fit in all the sightseeing and other activities you want to do. But, don't worry, you will – and you'll probably also find that you still have quite a lot of spare time on your hands. Spare time that you'll want to spend doing something, but preferably something that doesn't cost very much. Even when you're so bored you've already re-engineered the packing arrangement of your underwear, made a scale model of the Eiffel Tower from two-minute noodles and replied to that email from your great auntie about her triumph in the Women's Institute knitting competition, you still won't want to be paying out too much in the name of keeping yourself entertained. This chapter will help you avoid spending your evenings rearranging your underwear.

Then there are special occasions to be considered, times when you're looking for something just a little bit different to do – like Christmas, or your birthday. These days can be brilliant but can also be potentially homesickness-inducing, so here are some hints and tips on how to enjoy them.

DOING SOMETHING

Part of the point of backpacking is to see and experience different places and different cultures. It's not like living your normal life. Making the main focus of your existence sightseeing, cultural activities, long walks, adventure sports and copious amounts of drinking does take a bit of getting used to. It's a tough job but someone has to do it – and if you're on a long trip, that someone is you.

Sightseeing

What to see and do in any given place is the mainstay of your guidebooks – they'll identify the must-see places, alert you to the ones that are best avoided and point out the tackiest attraction in town – as will your fellow backpackers. If you're the kind of traveller who goes home disappointed if you haven't seen and done everything there is to see and do in a particular place, have a read through your guidebook before you arrive and plan your itinerary carefully to make sure you don't miss out. If you're a bit more relaxed, just see how the mood takes you, or wait till you get there and see what other people recommend.

Don't feel that you have to see absolutely everything, absolutely everywhere. You won't enjoy it if you're on a route march through every city and clock-watching your way through every place you visit. Just because your guidebook says something cannot be missed, that doesn't mean it cannot be missed. If it genuinely doesn't interest you but you go anyway just because it's the 'must-see' attraction, you'll probably find that it still doesn't interest you when you're there and you'll have wasted your time and money. Remember, too, that all good things have a saturation point. No matter how good the art is, how informative the museum is or how important the Buddhist temple is, there will come a point when you've seen enough art/museums/temples. Temple fatigue is a well-known phenomenon amongst travellers in Thailand, so don't feel bad if it happens to you. The clue that it's time to surrender is when you're more interested in the patterns the dust is making on your flip-flops than in what you've actually paid to see. And you don't always need to pay to see things. Sometimes sitting with a coffee and doing a bit of people watching, or going for a walk along the beach, or watching a sunset, is as much about absorbing the atmosphere of a place and gathering some amazing memories as visiting palaces, touring museums and going to cultural shows.

Adventure activities

To bungee or not to bungee, that will be the question. Especially if you're heading anywhere near the Antipodes, where anything involving excess adrenaline seems to be de rigueur in the backpacking world. On your travels, you'll be offered white water rafting, jet boats, zorbing, bungee, skydiving, paragliding, parascending, ballooning, quad biking, scuba diving, abseiling, go-karting, horse riding, climbing and canyoning, to name but a few. Where there are backpackers, it seems, there will be adventure activities.

Most of these activities you could do at home, but the point is that you never have. Somehow it seems to be a much better idea to do them in more exotic surroundings, as far away from your family as possible in order to ensure maximum impact in the worrying-your-mum-beyond-belief stakes and in a country where you'll have to pay for any medical treatment you might require as a result. And anyway, a bit like a truly terrible toilet story, the tale that starts 'When I did *my* skydive . . .', uttered in a tone of confident assumption that everyone listening to you will also have done a skydive, is one of the marks of a seasoned back-packer.

Right now you're probably thinking that you'll never do any of this stuff. Be warned – somehow the combination of sunshine and distance from home causes a weird chemical reaction in your brain. You start to think, hey, if I can travel round the world on my own I can so manage to jump out of a plane at 12,000 feet/throw myself off a high bridge attached to nothing but a thin rope of elastic/fly through the air supported only by a small piece of nylon. How hard can it be? This moment of clarity tends to last just long enough for you to book up the activity and get to the venue. Afterwards, you'll look back and be entirely unable to follow the logic of that train of thought and will once again fail to see the connection between travelling round the world and throwing yourself out of a plane. But by then, it'll be too late. You'll have parted with your hard-earned cash for less than a minute of scaring the hell out of yourself. But by then, you'll have done it. You'll have earned your backpacker spurs, and you'll be able to phone your mum, tell her what you've done and listen to her shriek. It's priceless.

I'm afraid that I can't offer you any advice on a bungee. I wasn't brave enough to do it. I did, however, do a skydive so I can help you with that. Just in case you're wondering how come I could do a skydive but I couldn't do a bungee, here's how it is. When you do a tandem skydive, you don't jump. You get pushed. You're strapped to a big bloke and he decides when you're going out of that plane. At that point, you have little choice other than to jump too. Conversely, when you do a bungee, *you* have to decide to jump. Crucial difference. But I digress; let's get back to the skydiving. It is an adrenaline rush, and it is an amazing thing to do. What's not so amazing is if your harness doesn't get fitted properly, because once the parachute deploys, the harness acts as a chair that you sit in for the rest of the fall. If it's not fitted properly, it cuts into your groin and thighs, and it's agony. Get it checked before you leave the ground, but if it does happen, there's not much you can do except grin and bear it and give thanks that you're not a bloke, because if you were, you probably wouldn't be having children after that. The other critical thing to remember about skydiving is breathing. Doesn't sound that hard now, but once you've jumped the air will be rushing into your face so fast that you won't be able to swallow any of it. Instead of gulping uselessly away like a fish out of water, just turn your head to the side as if you're swimming and coming up for air. Most importantly of all, remember that you can't scream and breathe at the same time. Stop screaming and start breathing.

CLIMBING SYDNEY HARBOUR BRIDGE FOR THE TERRIFIED

It is a bit expensive, but the experience of climbing Sydney Harbour Bridge is very special. For one thing, you simply can't do it anywhere else in the world. I didn't do the bridge climb the first time I went to Australia because I don't like heights and I didn't want to freak out in front of a bunch of strangers. I regretted it nearly as soon as I got home – not least because I didn't know if I'd ever go back there again to get another chance. So when I did, I knew I had to attempt the climb even though the thought of it, for me, was scarier than the skydive and scarier even than the ordeal of the Brazilian motorcycle taxi. I reasoned that at least if I tried it I'd know whether I could do it or not.

When I say I'm scared of heights, I don't actually mean that. What I mean is that I'm fine if there's a solid floor. It's floors I can see through that I have a problem with. Especially those metal mesh ones. And when you climb Sydney Harbour Bridge the first thing you have to do is complete a walkway suspended under the road deck of the bridge – made of, yes, you've guessed it, metal mesh. With a lovely view straight down to the sea below. At that, I very nearly bottled it before I even got to the bridge proper. However, I'd confessed to the guide that I was majorly scared so he was encouraging and reassuring – plus there were nine people behind me so going back wasn't an option without causing a scene. I gripped tight onto the handrail, kept looking straight ahead, took deep breaths and tried not to look down. There are some situations in life when it really is best not to look down. One is when a guy with a bald patch is performing cunnilingus on you, the other is when you're climbing Sydney Harbour Bridge. To my amazement, I was shaky, but it worked. Keep taking deep breaths, stop and stand still if you have to, and just take your time. It's worth it. Once you're on the bridge proper you get to climb on a nice, solid girder and the view is totally amazing.

Remember: fear is temporary, regret lasts forever.

Drinking

Drinking is a pretty big part of backpacker culture. When you can't afford food and you've been living on two-minute noodles for a week, you'll still somehow be able to find the money for a beer or two. Being a backpacker is a bit like being at uni – it's perfectly acceptable to spend far more on alcohol than you're prepared to spend on food. And, in any case, visiting bars and sampling the local rocket fuel definitely counts as an essential component of the whole cultural experience. How can you understand a country unless you understand what it drinks? There are vineyards to be visited in New Zealand, Australia and South Africa; tequila to be tasted in Mexico; caipirinhas to be consumed in Brazil; brewery tours to be braved the world over; gallons of cheap but very good *vino tinto* to be quaffed in Argentina; and you can't possibly leave Peru without getting totally piscoed on their fantastic national drink, the pisco sour. So get out there and indulge.

Certain places you'll visit are very enlightened about how much backpackers will spend on drinking and they're keen to capture some of that spend by offering you some great deals. The Antipodes are particularly good at this. Hunt about in any given town and you'll find hostelries offering discounts and special deals for backpackers. One of my personal favourites is in Taupo, New Zealand, where the bar staff will play paper-scissors-stone with you every round for a dollar off the drinks. And when you check in to your hostel in Queenstown, along with your room key you'll be issued with a weekly planner showing a timetable of all the happy hours in all the bars in town so that you can plan your evening's stagger for maximum alcohol, minimum spend.

Cusco goes one better. Since it's the gateway to the Inca Trail and therefore overrun with tourists with money to spend, the town has more than its fair share of bars and clubs, each desperate to pull in the trade. They do this by flooding the main square with touts bearing tickets for a free introductory drink. If you're smart, you can do the round of the square, collect a whole fistful of tickets and do a bar crawl, getting a free drink in each one. It'll usually be the roughest rum and coke ever mixed, but after about six it really doesn't matter any more. After 'doing the square run' you'll wake up with a hangover the size of Wales, vague memories of having snogged a bouncer and bruises from where you fell off the bar you were dancing on. (Or maybe that's just me, but I bet you'll end up with a similar story.)

THAT'S ENTERTAINMENT

No matter where in the world you go there is one certainty, and that certainty is an Irish bar. The Irish bar has made such a crusade of the world that it has managed to reach the parts that even McDonald's has been unable to reach. There are Irish bars in Bolivia, there are several Irish bars in Ushuaia (the town in Argentina known as the End of the World – you can get a stamp in your passport to prove it), and Cusco allegedly boasts the world's highest Irish bar. Just don't expect any of these bars to be remotely like a bar in Ireland. Calling an establishment an Irish bar seems to basically involve cutting some shamrocks out of a piece of green card, sticking them on the wall and serving a rough approximation of Guinness. Classy they are usually not, but if you're looking for the party in any given town in the world, they're a good starting point.

Other must-do activities for the high-heeled adventurer

Doing something scary, getting drunk for free in Cusco, pulling in an Irish bar and getting templed out in Thailand are all mainstays of the backpacker experience, but here are a few more things that you really should try if you find yourself in the right place in the world:

Get a massage: if you're visiting somewhere where a particular style of massage is part of the culture, frankly it would be rude not to give it a go, wouldn't it? For some low-cost pampering, take a Thai massage. It's a fairly public experience but, don't worry, you get to keep your clothes on. You'll be manipulated, creaking and cracking alarmingly, into positions you never thought you'd see outside of *More* magazine's 'Position of the Week' feature, but you'll feel very supple afterwards. For a much more private and intimate experience, take an Indian Ayurvedic massage. It is very relaxing but you'll need to leave your inhibitions at the door. In complete contrast to the Thais, Indian masseuses like you naked and covered in oil. Be prepared for a very thorough going over – as one of the girls I was travelling put it, she'd never before had her bum and her boobs massaged by someone she was paying to do it. Feel sorry for the boys – they get a masseur and we know how uncomfortable heterosexual men are about another man touching their bits.

Go to the cinema: sometimes it'll be the film that's the main attraction, other times it's the cinema itself. In Wanaka, New Zealand, you can sit back to watch the film from a selection of armchairs and sofas or even in half an old Morris Minor (the front half, so no shagging on the back seat, unfortunately). In Australia the cost-conscious backpacker can still get her fix of Hollywood hunks by taking advantage of Tight Arse Tuesday – when tickets are significantly cheaper than the rest of the week. Nasty name, nice concept. If you're in India, a cinema trip is essential to experience the brashness of Bollywood in its country of origin. You won't be able to understand a thing (except the random words of English with which it seems to be obligatory to pepper the dialogue of any given film) and there's no point in trying to follow the plot as it's only ever loosely strung together anyway. Bollywood doesn't need to tell a story, it just fills in the gaps between big song and dance numbers, as much cleavage as they dare risk showing and sex scenes which involve shots of bees and flowers rather than anyone actually getting down and dirty. If you happen to be in Jaipur, head to the cinema simply to see the venue. If you've never stood inside a wedding cake, now's your chance. The foyer's got layer upon layer of lavishly looped ice-white moulding, gilded crests and soft pink uplighting.

Sing karaoke in China: don't worry, it's not like at home. Here it's an art form. You'd don't have to sweat it in a bar and cross a dance floor the size of a football pitch in order to embarrass yourself in front of a crowd of strangers. Instead you get your own private room complete with sofa, microphones, big screen, disco lighting and a console to choose your songs. If you used to sing into your hairbrush in front of the mirror, now's your chance to grab the microphone. It's cheesy choon heaven. You can wail away all night to karaoke classics such as Abba, the Beatles, Steps and Madonna. I can particularly recommend the Bee Gees – the original tracks sound so highly improbable that it's virtually impossible to make them sound any worse than they did to start with. The performer in you will love it. It's such an amazing evening that you might find yourself dancing to 'Tragedy' or re-enacting THAT moment from *Titanic*. You might even discover that you appear to know all the lyrics to the Spice Girls' 'Wannabe' without having to look at the screen. Indulge yourself and don't worry about losing your dignity. Either get everyone else so plastered that they don't remember a thing about it in the morning or get them all to join in with 'Tragedy' so no one can say anything anyway.

DOs and DON'Ts *of sightseeing, scaring yourself and sampling the local brew*

- DO see what you want to see but don't force yourself to keep going once enough is enough. It is possible to see too many temples/museums/art galleries.
- DO feel free to miss a 'cannot-be-missed' attraction if it's just not your thing.
- DO be prepared to suddenly and uncharacteristically decide to do something really scary like jumping out of a plane or throwing yourself off a bridge.
- DO remember that when skydiving you can't scream and breathe at the same time.
- DON'T look down.
- DO take advantage of deals for cheap or free alcohol. It'd be rude not to and in any case, you're not going back, so it doesn't matter how much you embarrass yourself.
- DO do karaoke in China. Sing the Bee Gees and dance the 'Locomotion', indulge your inner child and forget about your street cred. You can always claim you were under the influence.
- DON'T feel bad about being a Tight Arse on a Tuesday. A girl's gotta do what a girl's gotta do to get a hit of cute silver screen stars.
- DO make the most of low-cost options for pampering yourself.

290

DOING NOTHING

To avoid spending your evenings rearranging your underwear, what you need are things to do which cost virtually nothing and fill in the gaps between actually travelling, seeing the sights and endangering your life in some adrenaline-fuelled activity. The ideal form of backpacker 'whiling away the hours' entertainment is one which a) costs nothing, b) doesn't take up valuable space in the backpack, and c) doesn't require presentable clothing. So here are some suggestions for how to kill time without killing yourself through boredom.

Talk to people — or listen to other people talking

Park up in the kitchen or in the bar and start listening to the conversations going on around you. Some of them are quite interesting in their own right and you could do worse than simply eavesdrop. If there's nothing amusing being discussed, try playing the 'guess the nationality' game for a bit and hone your recognition skills. If you find some Americans you can always have a bit of fun with them by asking them about geography, or try to get a French or German backpacker to pronounce the word 'Woolworths'. Once you get bored of that, try to engage someone in conversation. Practise your talking-to-strangers routine.

Play cards

Hostels the world over are full of people playing cards. After all, they're such a perfect way of passing long evenings; it costs nothing to play (unless you choose to bet on the games, but most backpackers don't), cards are easy to carry around, they don't take up much space in your backpack and there's no dress code required. You can even play cards on your own if there's no one to play with. (Yes, it is possible to play solitaire without a computer.) In short, cards are as close to perfect as a backpacker whiling-away-the-time option can get. That's IF you understand how to play. I don't. I'm pathologically incapable of remembering the rules for card games and have to have them explained to me in great detail, repeatedly, before and during the game. This makes me somewhat unpopular at a card table. Hopefully, however, you're better at this than me. If you either know the rules or have a memory that's better than a goldfish's, you'll be able to join in.

The two most popular games seem to be Uno and Arsehole/Shithead (the name of this latter game seems to vary according to how well the players know each other and whether anyone's mother or sister is involved). If you know (or can learn) how to play either or both of these games, you'll never be without something to do. You'll also find that by the end of your trip you're able to call someone an arsehole in about seven different languages. Possibly not something you thought you'd learn while travelling but you've got to admit it's a skill, and one which just might come in handy one day.

Backpacker card games are often accompanied by alcohol – usually of the cheap-wine-that-comes-out-of-a-cardboard-box sort, known to our Antipodean cousins as 'goon' (because they call the shiny silver bags inside those boxes 'goon bags'). It costs approximately £2.50 for four litres so it's right up there on the Great Backpacker Cost Saving Ideas list. Be warned. Goon is the only alcohol known to woman that tastes worse the more of it you drink. Be also warned that games which start as card games accompanied by a few mugs of goon (hostel kitchens rarely come stocked with wine glasses) have a habit of mutating into drinking games where excessive consumption of goon becomes the main activity of the evening. It's fun at the time but not so pretty the next morning. But hey, as long as you don't have to be on a bus by 5.30 a.m., why worry?

Read a book

Generally a solitary activity, so not quite as sociable as the card table, but still fulfilling the required criteria – fits easily in the backpack, requires minimum expenditure and can be done without feeling out of place while wearing scruffy, many-pocketed trousers and a T-shirt that you spilled red wine down three days ago. Reading will keep you busy at low cost and if you get a really good book the time will fly by.

While travelling you'll probably read things that you'd never have looked at twice at home. Ultimately, travelling for any period of time means some fairly random reading, because once you've finished the couple of books you brought with you from home, the best way to get more is to exchange – either with other travellers or from hostel book exchanges. The best thing about exchanging is that you never have to pay out for another book. You have to invest in the first couple but after that you can just keep on swapping. The worst thing is that your choice of reading material is limited to what's available to swap with.

Set your expectations of hostel book exchanges low and you'll not be disappointed. Some have a high-quality selection, with good choices. Occasionally, you might find an absolute treasure, something you've been wanting to read for ages, but at other times you'll just have to suck it and see. Wherever you are in the world, certain undeniable rules of existence seem to govern the book exchange. Much like there's always a teaspoon at the bottom of the bowl when you finish the washing up, any given hostel book exchange will always contain:

- One very dusty book in German which has clearly been lying there untouched for years – and, let's face it, if even the Germans find it boring, it must be.
- At least one romance of the 'Mills and Boon' style – if you've read one, you've read them all, but can be good for escapism.
- A fair amount of 'chick lit' (we seem to read more than the boys) – great if you're looking for something light for the beach but the problem might be finding something you've not already read.
- A dog-eared thriller with its cover missing – might be

a good read but check first whether all the pages are still there. It's really annoying if you start a good book then find out that the end is lost in action.

- Volume Four of a sci-fi series – totally useless unless you happen, perchance, to have read the preceding three (unlikely).

You'll also become familiar with the phenomenon of the Backpacker Book: the one which just about everyone seems to be reading. During my trip, *The Da Vinci Code* was one of these – my South American overland truck somehow spawned seven copies of it in three months – and another was *A Short History of Tractors in Ukrainian*. Then there are the country-specific reads. For example, anyone who is anyone backpacking in India has read *Are You Experienced?* and *Holy Cow!* whereas in Thailand *The Beach* is on everyone's reading list. If you're in a place where there's one of these books looming over everyone's heads you might as well accept the inevitable, get on with it and read it. At least then you can join in with the conversations.

DOs and DON'Ts for killing maximum time at minimum expense

- DO brush up on your card games before you leave home – and, if you want to stay ahead of the game, learn how to say 'shithead' in seven languages.
- DO approach life, love and reading with reckless abandon – it might not be what you'd read at home but try it, you might like it.

295

- DON'T get your hopes up about hostel book exchanges – that way if they do offer more than the dog-eared thriller, the useless sci-fi volume and something ancient and German you'll be pleasantly surprised.
- DON'T drink goon if you have to get up early the next day. No, not even one.
- DON'T try to fight against the one book that absolutely everybody is reading – bow to the inevitable.

SPECIAL OCCASIONS

If you're travelling for any length of time, some sort of occasion is bound to arrive while you're on the road. If you normally spend these with your family, you can be forgiven for feeling a little homesick at the prospect of being away from them. Sometimes you can recreate a celebration the way you'd have it at home, sometimes you can't. Sometimes you might not even want to. I have a Canadian friend who was totally up for making pumpkin pie for Thanksgiving, until she realized that in New Zealand they don't sell pumpkin pie filling in cans like they do in Canada and she'd have to start from scratch with cutting and stewing a fresh pumpkin.

My experiences of special occasions on the road have been a bit of a mixed bag – my birthday was amazing, Christmas was terrible, one New Year was jet-lagged and the other was frankly bizarre. Hopefully you'll get at least one good one. Here's how.

Your birthday

If you prefer to let your birthdays slide past without too much fuss, travelling will be perfect for you. If you're on the other side of the world with a bunch of strangers, no one is going to even know it's your birthday, never mind make a fuss about it. However, if you like to feel special on your birthday, a little bit of forward planning may be required. Have a think about how you want to spend the day. Maybe you want to be partying with a bunch of other people, maybe you want to treat yourself by booking into a spa and pampering yourself or maybe you want to do a particular activity that day? Take a good look at your itinerary and plan to be somewhere on your birthday where you can do what you want to do on the day.

If you're going to be with a tour group, plan to join the tour a little bit before your birthday so that your fellow travellers have a chance to get to know you. They'll be more inclined to make an effort for your birthday if they do – and they will. I'd only known my South American tour group for a few weeks when my birthday rolled around but they cooked me fajitas and shared with me an evening in hot pools under the stars and lots of bottles of pink champagne. If you're not the tour type but you want people around on your birthday, select a likely-looking town in which to celebrate your birthday and arrive a few days in advance to give yourself time to get to know a few people and check out the best bars. Most backpackers will be up for a party so let it be known it's your birthday and the party will probably follow you. If being in touch with family and friends at home is important to you, try to make sure you'll be staying somewhere with Internet access or a telephone. If you have the address of wherever you're going to be staying on your birthday, give it to your family and friends well in advance so they can send you birthday cards and maybe a little treat – some of your favourite toiletries, a top-up pot of Marmite or maybe a new book.

Your birthday is the perfect excuse to break the budget. Treat yourself to a nice meal out, book a single room at the hostel, buy a bottle of wine instead of a box. If you're going to be somewhere remote like the Aussie outback where heading for a good restaurant isn't going to be an option, buy up some special food and drink before you leave civilization to carry with you and have on the day. It'll give you something to look forward to. And remember, when you're backpacking, a good meal really can make your day. To make it truly feel like a birthday, get some birthday cake candles and stick them in something so you can blow them out. If not a big cake then how about a cupcake, or even a piece of fruit or a pizza?

DEATH BY CREAM CAKE

On my South American tour, by the time my birthday came around I had some idea what to expect and I was worried. There had been other birthday celebrations, all involving the birthday girl or boy having their face

---

pushed into a cake. Quite gently, admittedly, usually resulting in cream on the nose and chin, but cake in the face nevertheless. I wasn't looking forward to this. I've always had a vague distrust of clowns and even as a small child I never found the whole custard pie routine funny. Gross, yes, but funny? Having a cream cake shoved in my face was fairly high on my list of things I could happily go to my grave without ever having experienced and not feel like I'd missed out. However, since I knew it was on the cards I psyched myself up to grin and bear it. Or at least not to lose it and scream at everyone.

Right on cue after dinner, the cake appeared. The cake deliverer vigorously shoved the cake upwards just as someone standing behind me vigorously shoved my head downwards. The result was a cake and face sandwich; cream up my nose, cream in my mouth, cream in my eyes, cream in my hair and cream all down my front. I raised my head. There was total silence. Everyone was wondering if they'd gone too far and how I was going to react. I surprised myself. I laughed. I laughed and laughed. I laughed so hard that I quite literally nearly died from suffocation as I inhaled cream from every orifice. Most surprisingly of all, it was actually funny.

If this should happen to you, try to take it well. You'll be able to hold your head up high, prove that you can take a joke. The clean-up operation is slightly less dignified as you dig the cream out of your mouth and nostrils (I'd recommend doing that quickly so you can breathe again). Get someone else to wipe it all off your face and out of your hair. When it happened to me, I was luckily wearing my waterproof jacket, which of course is basically wipe-clean.

Handy hint: if you think you might end up with cake on your face, you could do worse than spend your birthday wearing waterproofs.

Christmas

The thing about Christmas, as distinct from your birthday, is that everyone will be celebrating it; it's not unique to you. Theoretically this should mean that it will be easier to get everyone into the party spirit. Unfortunately, it also might mean that everyone will be homesick at the same time. Again, a bit of forward planning will help. As with your birthday, stock up on some special food or drink for the day. If you're going to be with a group of people, organize a present exchange – give people a fair bit of notice and set a spending limit. Some hostels and some tour leaders will make an effort for Christmas, while others won't, so don't rely on someone else. Bake a cake or cook a special dinner – at least you'll feel like you did something even if no one else does. Load some Christmas tunes onto your iPod, or sing carols to get in the Christmas spirit. Sing them in the shower if you don't want to sing them in front of other people. If you can, arrange to be staying with a family over Christmas as it feels so much more homely than a hostel. Crash at a relative's or stay with friends. Alternatively, take a wwoofing placement a couple of weeks before Christmas and stay on.

Even if you don't end up having the best-ever Christmas, console yourself with the thought that your Christmas on the road is unlikely to be as tragic as mine was. I spent it in an African game reserve during unseasonal heavy rains with a leaking tent and a leaking truck and no game viewing (due to the rain). To top it all, Christmas dinner was cold pasta (left over from the night before) and sausages. I even started to miss Brussels sprouts, which I normally have to be forced to eat 'because it's tradition'. On the plus side, we did at least have a mobile phone signal so we could get goodwill messages from home and I had stashed a bottle of Amarula Cream in my backpack so I spent the afternoon getting pleasantly plastered in my tent while listening to the rain gently falling on the canvas.

New Year's Eve

Have you ever had more than one good New Year's Eve? I'm fairly sure that no one has. It usually ends up being a lot of hype over nothing, paying a fortune to get in somewhere that isn't that great anyway and then drinking yourself sober. The good thing is that whatever happens on your new year on the road it's unlikely to be worse than it normally is, and it might even be better. For a start, if you're anywhere within the southern hemisphere the chances are it'll be hot. And new year on a beach has to beat shivering your way through a midnight conga down your great-aunt's road, doesn't it? Most people celebrate new year so finding a crowd to hook up with and drink to excess with at any given hostel or campsite shouldn't be all that challenging. Unlike Christmas or your birthday, there's no special food to miss or traditions to mark (except perhaps singing 'Auld Lang Syne', and you can do that anywhere – assuming, of course, that you know the words), so that makes it all so much easier straight away.

My first new year away from home (in New Zealand) was

slightly mistimed since I'd landed only a couple of days earlier and was still jet-lagged, but there was a good crowd at the hostel, fireworks on the beach and I just about made it past midnight before succumbing to the jet-lag and collapsing into bed. My second new year away from home arrived in Arusha, Tanzania, on the ill-fated safari. Knowing that you have to get up at 5 a.m. the next day to go on a long drive in the back of a leaking truck with no suspension does slightly dampen your enthusiasm for drinking excess alcohol, especially when it's rough-as-guts African beer, so instead a small crowd of us sat on plastic patio furniture at our 'motel' watching the clock on someone's phone click past midnight, sang 'Auld Lang Syne', wished each other a happy new year and headed off to bed. Not exactly rock and roll but memorable nevertheless. And, let's face it, however your new year turns out, it's probably not going to be much worse than what you usually end up doing, is it?

DOs and DON'Ts for making special occasions special

- DO start out with low expectations – it makes it harder to be disappointed.
- DO plan ahead. Hoard some good food and drink, plan to be with a group of people you know (or will have at least spent a bit of time with by then) or book something special as a treat.
- DO arrange to be somewhere with Internet and/or telephones if you want to be in touch with home on the big day.

- DON'T wait for someone else to make the effort – get on in there and make it happen.
- DO wear waterproofs if you think there's a chance you might end up with your face in a cake.
- DO sing in the shower if it'll get you in the festive spirit.
- DON'T worry if you start to miss Brussels sprouts – it'll pass.
- DO look on the bright side – if you have a really terrible birthday or Christmas, the next one you have at home will be even better in comparison.

Suggested Packing List

Just in case you haven't managed to track down a packing list anywhere else, here are my suggestions of things to take with you – but remember, think about where you're going and what you'll need for the activities you want to do.

Basics – clothes and shoes:

- Jeans
- Zip-off lightweight trousers (1 or 2 pairs)
- Shorts (1 or 2 pairs)
- T-shirts (3 or 4)
- Skirt
- Top for going out
- Sarong (not a waterproof one!)
- Swimwear (2 items)
- Sun hat
- T-shirt to swim in
- Fleece and/or jumper
- Hat and gloves
- Thermal vest
- Something to wear in bed
- Waterproof jacket

- Underwear
- Hiking socks
- Walking boots or shoes
- Rubber flip-flops
- Strappy sandals, small heels or other going-out shoes, such as sparkly flip-flops

Basics – other items:

- Passport and tickets
- Guidebooks
- Credit card and cash card
- Travel insurance certificate
- Photocopies of passport and other important documents
- Driving licence
- Sleeping bag and liner
- Head torch
- Travel towels
- First-aid kit
- Reusable water bottle
- Travel wash
- Travel plug adaptor
- Toiletries and make-up
- Insect repellent
- Suncream
- Small selection of jewellery
- Medication
- Condoms
- Tampons
- Nail scissors and emery board

SUGGESTED PACKING LIST

- Ear plugs
- Eye mask
- Money belt, elastic bandage or similar
- Padlocks (at least 2)
- Compass
- Umbrella
- Travel alarm clock
- Rechargeable batteries and charger
- Camera, memory cards, batteries or battery pack and leads for downloading
- Binoculars (if you're going to be doing a lot of bird or wildlife watching)
- Sunglasses
- Pens
- Small notebook
- Reading books
- Mobile phone and charger
- Small bag for dirty laundry
- Net 'packing cube' to keep underwear together
- Universal plug for sinks

Additionally, if you're going to be doing a lot of camping and/or hiking, you might also need:

- Waterproof trousers
- Washing line
- Penknife
- Travel wash

- Sewing kit
- Small dry bag
- Sleeping mat
- Tent
- Mosquito net
- Small squashy pillow (also useful if you're going to be spending a lot of time on cheap trains with hard seats)
- Cutlery, saucepans, bowl, plate and mug

Things to Do Before You Go

These are my suggestions of the main things you'll probably want to do before you head off on your travels. But don't panic if you're being impulsive and you've booked your ticket less than three months in advance – you can still do it all, you'll just be a lot busier!

First things:
- Book your ticket
- Buy your travel insurance

Three months to go:
- Visit your GP or travel clinic to find out what jabs you need (remember to take your itinerary with you) and then schedule them in
- Start thinking about your preferred method of contraception while travelling and make the necessary arrangements with your GP, whether it's having something fitted or stockpiling the Pill
- Buy hiking boots or walking shoes if needed and start wearing them in
- Give notice on your place if you rent

Two months to go:

- Start doing your research about what kit you need and what options are available – get packing lists from your travel agent, travel stores or the Internet
- Start writing lists
- Continue wearing in your walking boots
- Check out whether your bank charges for cash withdrawals abroad. If it does, investigate options for accounts which don't charge and open one of those
- Organize a big night out with your mates for just before you go
- Find out what visas you need for your trip (if any) and apply for them

One month to go:

- Resign from work
- Go to your tax office to collect relevant tax forms or visit the HM Customs and Revenue website to download them (worth doing this – you might get a bit of a tax refund)
- Buy all your kit (don't forget your head torch, and do not get a waterproof sarong!)
- Keep wearing in those boots
- Organize for your mum or someone else you trust to have third-party access to your bank accounts and credit card so that they can sort stuff out if anything goes wrong while you're away
- Buy all your guidebooks (or even better, get people to give them to you as presents)

310

- Start researching blog sites if you want to do one while you're away
- Set up Internet banking if you don't already have it
- Cancel any magazine subscriptions or anything else you don't need while you're away

Two weeks to go:
- Do a trial pack
- Make sure your boots are fully worn in
- Transfer your travel money to the bank account you want to use when you're abroad
- Get your blog up and running
- Contact the Post Office and redirect your mail if you're moving out

One week to go:
- Check with your travel agent and airline that everything is OK for your departure
- Notify your car insurance that you want to cancel it from your date of departure
- Get some local currency for your first stop
- Photocopy your passport, driving licence, insurance documents and any other important stuff you're taking with you and leave one copy of it all with your mum
- Make sure you have all the medication you need to take with you
- Compile a distribution list in your email account so you can easily send updates to your friends and family as you're travelling

- Start packing if you're moving out of somewhere and storing your stuff while you're away

Three days to go:

- Get your hair cut, get everything waxed, get a fake tan and, if needed, get semi-permanent make-up applied
- Stock up on condoms and tampons
- Put all the clothes you want to take with you through the wash
- Give your mum a copy of your itinerary so she doesn't have to worry about where you are

Two days to go:

- Purchase any food you want to take with you, like chocolate or Marmite
- Move all your stuff into storage if you need to

One day to go:

- Declare your car off road (if you've got somewhere off road to park it while you're away – that way you don't have to pay road tax on it). You can do this online at the DVLA website
- Pack – for real this time
- Eat your favourite meal
- See all your friends and family
- Get excited

Index

Page ranges in **bold** denote complete chapters

boots, walking 16, 26, 28, 218, 306
  wearing in 309, 310, 311
  see also footwear
bra, as carrier 153, 161, 166, 225,
  248
Brazil 93, 162–3, 201, 227, 285
bucket showers 109–10
buying toothpaste in Argentina
  249–53

cameras 257, 307
  backing up photos 263
  carrying 11, 160, 162, 163
  secure storage of 159
camping 12, 259
  clothes for 18, 28–9
  and food 77, 84–5
  and hygiene 123–4
  shops 9, 10, 35
  and washing 84–5, 106–8, 115
Canada 71, 77, 150–1, 229, 231
  accent of 214, 215–16
cards, credit and debit 306, 310
  fraud risk 247
  security of 111, 159–61, 166
cars 45, 311
  declaring off-road 312
  driving 202–4
  hiring 202
cash 310
  access to 159–60, 161, 166
  machines 246–9
China 78, 126–7, 151, 227
  cultural differences in 219–20,
  226

food in 90, 92, 95–6
internet access in 267–8
karaoke in 289–90
pedestrians in 198–9, 204–5
scams in 164, 166
train travel in 194, 198
see also Beijing
cleanliness and hygiene 63,
  105–30
  in hostel kitchens 82
clothes 186
  packing 16–21, 42–3, 305–6
  suitablitiy of 9, 145, 170–1
  washing 11, 114–21
communicating with home
  257–75
compass 33–5, 46, 164, 193
condoms
  availability of 30–1, 253, 312
  and health 152–3, 154, 225
cooking 86–7
  and camping 12, 77
  in hostels 53–4, 79–83, 91
  for others 84–5
  see also food
cultural differences 40–1, 198–9,
  219–20, 270–5, 280–1
Cusco, Peru 89, 286, 287
customs officials 137, 138, 165,
  216–18, 226

dating 224–6
daypack 11, 160, 192
doctors 31, 138, 144
  and contraception 143

INDEX

Acknowledgements

I would like to thank everyone who has helped me to realize my dream and get this book published. Special thanks must go to Nicki Clark and Becky Whale, for reading the early drafts and providing helpful comments and suggestions for improvement; Camilla Bolton, for timely advice and encouragement; David Fulcher, for reminding me that boys don't need to be told how to pee in the bush; my agent, Susan Smith, and my editor, Lorraine Green, for their invaluable suggestions, assistance and enthusiasm, as well as the patience to answer all my silly questions; and all my friends and family who read my emails, smiled and encouraged me to keep writing. I should also thank all my fellow travellers for making my journeys interesting, entertaining and, above all, memorable – especially those who sang karaoke with me in China, fellow survivors of the safari from hell, staff and volunteers at GVI South Africa and, of course, the Jocks from South America (particularly the Tintettes) – Trevor is most definitely a bus.

Visit **www.panmacmillan.com** to read more about all our books and to buy them. You will also find features, author interviews and news of any author events, and you can sign up for e-newsletters so that you're always first to hear about our new releases.